PRAISE FOR DRINK LIKE A GEEK

"Listen, I like James Bond. And I like *Star Wars*. But I love drinking. And when this book made it clear that I could fully combine a series of films with a series of drinks, I ascended straight to heaven. Not only is Cioletti's book informative and inventive, but wildly entertaining as well. Of course, I'm drunk on an Ewok 'Bright Tree Swizzle,' but there you go."

—Matt Gourley, actor, comedian, & co-host of the *James Bonding* and *Superego* podcast

"Jeff is a geek, but he's no snob. Like a friend who lends favorite comic books or tips you off to a great IPA, this book opens up new worlds and shares your passion for their minute details. *Drink Like A Geek* revels in nerd culture while remembering that the best parts of being in the club are the people—and drinks—there with you."

—Kate Bernot, managing editor, The Takeout (TheTakeout.com)

"A geek's geek and a drinker's drinker, Jeff Cioletti authoritatively puts a whole spectrum of geek-loved media together with peppy, name-checked cocktails. Wonderfully unique! Get Boilermakers with good old Greedo, and see who shoots first. Drink Romulan Ale with Doc McCoy, Tardis-blue gin with The Doctor, and a corrected Vesper with Bond, James Bond. Then argue about them; that's what Geeks do."

—Lew Bryson, Author of *Tasting Whiskey* and *Whiskey Master Class*; senior drinks writer at The Daily Beast

"You know that line about booze and knowledge? I'm convinced Tyrion Lannister stole it from Jeff Cioletti. The author of this book has an unabashed love and appreciation for inventive drinks and all forms of geekery. The two have more in common than you might think, and, as both step in from the fringes, Cioletti is here to get you deeper into your favorite genre and glass."

—John Holl, author of *Drink Beer, Think Beer: Getting to the Bottom of Every Pint* and co-host of *Steal This Beer*, a podcast

DRINK LIKE A GEEK

For permission requests, please contact the publisher at:
Mango Publishing Group
2850 S Douglas Road, 2nd Floor
Coral Gables, FL 33134 USA
info@mango.bz

For special orders, quantity sales, course adoptions and corporate sales, please email the publisher at sales@mango.bz. For trade and wholesale sales, please contact Ingram Publisher Services at customer.service@ingramcontent.com or +1.800.509.4887.

Drink Like a Geek: Cocktails, Brews, and Spirits for the Nerd in All of Us

Library of Congress Cataloging-in-Publication number: 2019941803
ISBN: (print) 978-1-64250-011-0, (ebook) 978-1-64250-012-7
BISAC category code: CKB088000 COOKING / Beverages / Alcoholic / General

Printed in the United States of America

DRINK LIKE A GEEK

Cocktails, Brews, and Spirits for the Nerd in All of Us

JEFF CIOLETTI

Author of *The Year of Drinking Adventurously*
and *The Drinkable Globe*

To my wife, Craige. Guess what—you married a nerd!

TABLE OF CONTENTS

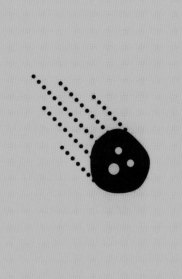

INTRODUCTION
WORLDS COLLIDE

I've always felt equally at home in the sci-fi/fantasy realm and the drinking world, but I must admit, my first experience connecting these two domains was that of an interloper.

It was Labor Day weekend, 1998. I was in Atlanta for Dragon Con, one of the largest genre conventions in the country. Over the years, as more such events have proliferated across the US and the world, the Georgia celebration has retained its reputation as the more raucous, less corporate, party-animal cousin to Hollywood-centric gatherings like the San Diego Comic-Con. It's still showbiz, but Dragon Con, unlike many of its ilk, continues to be more "show" than "biz."

At Dragon Con's 1998 event, *Star Wars* fans—among whom I enthusiastically count myself—were giddy with anticipation for the arrival of *Episode I*, which was still nearly nine months away. It wasn't even *The Phantom Menace* then because that title had yet to be announced. The possibility that a *Star Wars* movie could suck seemed unlikely. The prequel trilogy represented hope and possibility. The films were far from becoming the sad punchline that they are now.

As part of the *Star Wars* generation—I was five, eight, and eleven when the originals played in cinemas—I was so excited for a brand-new era in the space opera franchise that had defined my youth that I decided to capture fans' anticipation for the prequels in my first documentary film, *Millennium's End: The Fandom Menace*. I started shooting in the late summer of 1997—nearly two years before *Episode I*'s May 1999 release date—and a year into the project, I was preparing for what would be the most intense three days of production.

If geekdom seems fairly tribal to folks on the outside looking in, it's even more so to those within it. Each genre property of any significance—be it *Star Wars*, *Star Trek*, *Doctor Who*, or *Lord of the Rings*—has its own rabid fan base. The more passionate members of those bases usually stick close to their own tribes. Sure, there's some border crossing going on because people tend to have multiple interests. However, there was, at least in those days, one universal truth: You were either a *Star Wars* person or a *Star Trek* person. You had to choose a side. No exceptions.

Each major property had its own "track" at Dragon Con, and each track got its own conference room in which to schedule events throughout the long weekend. A local group called Matters of the Force managed the *Star Wars* programming at the convention. The room became my de facto base of operations for the duration of the four-day con. However, that doesn't mean I didn't venture out into other areas.

The *Trek* room was two or three doors down, and I was enticed by the prospect of hanging out behind enemy lines. Okay, it was really the free booze. I experienced a bit of cognitive dissonance because the Trekkies hosting the soiree turned out to be some of the most welcoming, hospitable folks I'd encountered at the Con. Most of them were decked out in full Klingon prosthetics and regalia—I'm not talking cheesy, store-bought Halloween costumes here. We're talking Hollywood quality, and most of their wardrobe and accoutrements were completely homemade. Some of the Trekkies had spent the better part of a year tailoring their outfits. You've got to respect that kind of commitment.

As I entered the room that Rodenberry Built (not really, but it has a nice ring, no?), a greeter handed me a Solo cup full of a curious blue liquid.

"Here, enjoy some Romulan Ale," he said.

My ambivalence kicked in for a moment. I mean, to a *Star Wars* fan, sipping such forbidden nectar was akin to drinking the blood of Satan. Okay, maybe that's a bit extreme. It was more like a member of the Busch family drinking a Coors Light.

It was a pretty inoffensive concoction that alternated between moderately sweet and assertively tart. Perhaps the sour, multi-colored gummy worm sitting at the bottom of the cup enhanced the more pucker-inducing aspects. I still have the video footage of my first sip.

The fact that I'm recalling the experience more than two decades later speaks to the indelible mark the moment left on my psyche.

No, it didn't make me a Trekkie (okay, Trek*er*). But it did give me a greater appreciation for passions that weren't necessarily my own. And it also gave me a bit of a bone to pick with my *Star Wars* compatriots. They really needed to up their booze game. After all, one of the saga's most iconic scenes took place in a bar (where Han did, indeed, shoot first!) and the only thematically correct liquid that most disciples of Lucas were drinking circa 1998 was whole milk with blue food coloring. (If that reference is lost on you, go rewatch the scenes at Owen and Beru Lars's Tattooine moisture farm in *Episode IV: A New Hope*.)

Thankfully, a great deal has changed. Now there are entire bars that transport guests to a galaxy far, far away and breweries crafting beers like "It's a Trap IPA" and "That's No Moon."

It was such developments that made me realize that my two passions—booze and genre nerdery—had evolved in parallel. Craft beer, high-end spirits, and classic cocktails had entered the modern zeitgeist at about the same time that Comic-Cons and all of the pop culture properties in their orbit had moved out of the parents' basements and into the mainstream. Even better, *Doctor Who*, the British TV show that shaped my adolescence until it was unceremoniously cancelled by the BBC while I was in high school, was finally being properly resurrected (half-hearted 1996 TV movie notwithstanding) sixteen years after it left screens seemingly forever. By the mid-2000s, the planets were finally aligning.

Being a nerd was suddenly cool. If I jumped into a TARDIS and traveled back to 1984 to reveal that twenty-first-century truth to my twelve-year-old self—well, the little brat would probably steal my TARDIS and leave me stranded in the Reagan era, but you get where I'm going with this.

Around that same time, beer festivals, spirits tastings, and general beverage trade shows started to outnumber sci-fi conventions on my calendar. After screening *Millennium's End* at San Diego Comic-Con in 2000, I had something of an open invitation to showcase future projects there. I would screen three more geeky documentaries there, as well as a couple of spoofy, *Star Wars*-related comedy shorts over the next four years. By then, though, the Hollywood establishment had already begun to descend on Comic-Con and it became impossible to schedule anything if you weren't employed by a major studio.

The iconic San Diego festival wouldn't be the last convention at which I'd screen a nerd-themed production. In 2005, I shot a sequel to my first documentary called *Galaxy's End: Revenge of the Myth*, revisiting most of the same fans interviewed in the late '90s and sort of bookending the prequel fan experience. I hadn't planned it at the time, but when I premiered it at the inaugural New York Comic Con in 2006, it served as a similar bookend to my fandom-related filmmaking. My audiovisual attention had started to turn toward drinks. In 2007, I started kicking around an idea for a script about a bar that transforms itself into a church of beer, when suddenly, the town it is in goes dry. I wrote and tweaked it over the next year and a half, and in the summer of 2009, my filmmaking partner, Lou Tambone, and I shot *Beerituality*. It premiered a year later.

Since then, I've continued to make films of sorts—in the form of mini, documentary-style booze-and-travel videos for my website, DrinkableGlobe.com. But lately, I've been spending more time typing at a laptop (too often staring at a blank page) than I have been stressing out behind a camera. Meanwhile, I've felt a gentle tug back into the genre geek realm, professionally speaking. (I never left as a fan, just creatively.) It probably began with a piece I wrote on nerdy breweries for *All About Beer* magazine in 2015. In that article, I observed how craft beer culture and Comic-Con culture went mainstream and became big business simultaneously. A similar revolution in distilled spirits and cocktails started to pick up steam at around the same time. In my mind, this was no coincidence.

And in my mind, this time it felt as if leaving one world didn't have to happen at the expense of the other. It was like both worlds caught up with each other and now have caught up with me. I hope you enjoy playing in the booze nerd and genre geek sandboxes as much as I do. And you'll never have to feel like an interloper in either.

CHAPTER 1
THE SAGA BEGINS IN A BAR

She may not look like much, but she's got enough to drink for several people.
Photo credit: Jeff Cioletti (special thanks to Beeline Creative)

Forget about Darth Vader and the garrison of Stormtroopers blasting their way onto the Tantive IV. Stick a pin in the scene where R2-D2 and C-3PO peace out on an escape pod with Princess Leia's stolen Death Star plans in tow. Fast-forward through the Droids meeting Luke, the Tusken Raider attack, and the Owen and Beru Barbecue, and you'll get to the place where the *Star Wars* saga really begins (prequels notwithstanding).

It's in the Mos Eisley Cantina where the *Star Wars* galaxy suddenly gets bigger. Up to that point, we'd met both the forces of good and of evil. But in the bar, we encounter the forces of gray—not the least of those is a certain Correllian smuggler who ultimately becomes so popular that he gets his own spinoff origin movie. (And, yes, he shot first.)

It's a powder keg of a Wild West saloon. The proprietors do their best to keep the place from exploding—a live jazz band is a calming distraction—but the events of that fateful afternoon prove that place really is hanging by a thread. In the space of about ten minutes, an old man in a brown robe unceremoniously amputates the arm of one paying customer and a surly, vest-wearing pilot guns down another.

On a good day, it's the place where deals are made, secret alliances are forged and beings from a thousand worlds seek to disappear into anonymity—"No questions asked," remember? And it all happens over drinks. When relations do go south—as they did on the day in question—it's despite the imbibing, not because of it.

The Cantina may not always advance the case for social drinking occasions—thanks, Han—but the famous interstellar public house accomplished in a few quick wide, medium, and close-up shots what it often takes franchises multiple movies to establish: that the *Star Wars* universe was huge and there were millions of stories waiting to be told. Up until that point in the film, we were introduced to some of the galaxy's exotic species in a very gradual, rationed manner. We met the Jawas and then the Tusken Raiders, but not until we got to Mos Eisley did we behold the vastness of the galaxy.

All the more remarkable is the fact that George Lucas accomplished that with a reported budget of around eleven million dollars. Sure, that's in mid-1970s dollars, but if you adjusted it for inflation, it'd still be only about forty-five million. That is the average price of an effects-free comedic film, half of which would be the salary of the A-list star.

Scenes from Jabba's palace. Photo credit: Jeff Cioletti (special thanks to Beeline Creative)

That's the magic of a bar. In the real world, it's like life's great establishing shot, offering a glimpse at a wide cross-section of humanity in such a confined space. Why do you think Yelp reviews always tout "great people-watching" at different venues? (Though, why is people-watching even a thing?)

Maz Kenata's thousand-year-old watering hole in *The Force Awakens* and the Canto Bight casino in *The Last Jedi* also serve this purpose, though we don't feel their impact as much as we did when we first heard the first notes of John Williams's jazzy cantina band number (we later learn that seven-member musical combo was Figrin D'an and the Modal Nodes—"Fiery" Figrin D'an and his cohorts were members of the Bith race).

"There's always that collective shot, that collective starting point," observes Atlanta-based *Star Wars* fan photographer and social media consultant Brett Ferencz. "Whether it's Maz's, the Cantina, or the Casino, there's always these massive collections of aliens and strange characters. It's a great representation of how vast the world is that they're creating."

SCOTCH TROOPER

Ferencz's name may not seem that familiar, but his Instagram alter ego is practically a household name in spirits-drinking circles: Scotch Trooper. His expertly composed images typically show *Star Wars* action figures interacting in some way with bottles, barrels, and glasses of whisk(e)y.

Scotch Trooper (Scotch_Trooper on Instagram) evolved from Ferencz's earlier efforts to showcase his newfound passion for the spirit. Initially, he fell in love with the shapes of the bottles and the way the light played off of them. "I would use a lot of the empty bottles that I was holding on to that were just too pretty to throw away," Ferencz recalls. "My wife said you should probably throw them away or do something with them—you're just cluttering up the house."

He then turned a lot of those bottles into steampunk-ish lamps and showed them off on Instagram. That's when things started to take off. The number of followers quickly jumped to ten thousand. "That was 2015 or so, and that was my first step into the industry," he says, "I started getting noticed by brand ambassadors."

It was also around that time that he decided to more prominently integrate his other passion with the images: *Star Wars*. "I remember being five years old, wearing my Ewok shirt, and seeing *Return of the Jedi* with my neighbor," Ferencz says of his near-lifelong fandom. "Every birthday party from then on had a *Star Wars* theme."

He started incorporating standard 3¾-inch Hasbro figures in his posts but quickly realized that those figures lacked the proportions he wanted for his photos. He moved on to six-inch figures, which worked perfectly. "And that's also when I brought in my Nikon camera and upgraded the photography," Ferencz reveals. "And then it kind of blew up." Impressed by his unique images, The *Huffington Post* did a profile on Scotch Trooper, and his following increased even further. Major whiskey brands began to partner with him to showcase their bottles in Ferencz's *Star Wars*-themed scenes. One of his images included Princess Leia sitting down for a drink with *Rogue One* heroine Jyn Erso, with a giant bottle of Lagavulin looming in the background. Another featured a pair of original trilogy-era Stormtroopers, a bottle of Talisker Skye, and a skateboarding Yoda.

A couple years later, Ferencz hit a major speed bump in the spring of 2018 when the Distilled Spirits Council, the trade association representing America's large distillers and importers, sent him a cease and desist order. The organization had no problem with his sponsored relationships with its member companies. However, the Council did object to his use of action figures. The trade group had received an anonymous, twenty-six-page complaint asserting that Scotch Trooper violated the Distilled Spirits Council's advertising code, which states that the expected audience for a print, broadcast, or digital ad (which includes social media), must be at least 71.6 percent of legal drinking age. The Council's Code Review Board determined that the use of action figures targets children.

Except it doesn't. Ferencz posted the demographic analytics of his Instagram traffic and 90 percent of his followers (which have climbed past sixty-five thousand) are twenty-five and older. Less than 1 percent are teenagers between thirteen and seventeen years old, and 10 percent are eighteen to twenty-four years old. More than half of that last group are of legal drinking age. So, the total number of legal drinking age followers is probably closer to 95 percent—exceeding the Distilled Spirits Council's minimum threshold by nearly twenty-four percentage points!

Naturally, the decision caused Ferencz to lose a huge chunk of his livelihood. However, he has been able to slowly rebuild to some extent, picking up a couple of deals with smaller brands far from the Distilled Spirits Council's reach.

"Scotch Trooper is still kind of a moving target," Ferencz says. "Scotch Trooper was one thing and that really opened the doors working with brands on the side—social media management, freelance photography, consultant stuff. This whole [Distilled Spirits Council issue] didn't just kill what was going on the Scotch Trooper side."

This is pretty personal for me too. I'm well into my forties, and I still collect action figures. A lot of other people my age and older do as well. We're the *Star Wars* generation—Gen Xers who grew up with the original trilogy. We're a nostalgic lot. And now, a lot of us happen to drink whisk(e)y as well. We haven't traded one hobby for the other. And that's why Scotch Trooper has been so successful. We're excited to see millennials and the up-and-coming Generation Z getting as stoked about some of these franchises as we are.

"The reason my account blew up the way it did, at least in my eyes, is that the people who grew up with *Star Wars* are now at that prime age for getting into whiskey, for getting into spirits in general," Ferencz notes. "Being able to see characters they grew up loving interacting with the spirits they're now getting into—it really kind of catapulted what I was doing, that perfect marriage."

There's really not much of a difference between the passion that drives *Star Wars* fans and the passion that fuels whisk(e)y aficionados.

"A geek who gets into *Star Wars* and dives into finding everything out about characters and their origins is very similar to the way we look at whiskey," he explains. "It's not just a spirit we drink to get drunk with friends. We dive into everything about distilleries, find out what barley they're using, what kind of casks are being married in and the differences between those. There are so many different elements to dive into, so it makes that perfect connection between the two."

DARTH MALT

If this book were a game show, this would be the speed round. I asked Ferencz to come up with the right whiskies to pair with particular moments throughout the Star Wars saga. (And, yes, that includes the prequels. Sorry!)

CLASSIC TRILOGY

A New Hope: The Cantina

The iconic watering hole in Tattooine's port city of Mos Eisley is everything you'd expect it to be: gritty, sleazy, and more than a little bit dangerous.

Since the Cantina is essentially the Wild West, Ferencz thinks a "cheap-ass bourbon" would be the drink of choice. I am on board for that. His suggestion is kind of refreshing since so much of today's bourbon consumption is about high-priced connoisseurship. Sometimes it's okay to drink like a cowboy. So, pour yourself a glass of Old Granddad and immerse yourself in that "wretched hive of scum and villainy."

Empire Strikes Back: Darth Vader's Bespin Banquet

Vader would be honored if you would join him for a few glasses of the lightly peated Compass Box No Name Blended Scotch. "This is exactly where my mind went when you said 'Darth Vader,'" Ferencz says. "It's a very Vader-ish bottle." Indeed it is. The label is an opaque black.

Return of the Jedi: Post-Battle of Endor Celebration

You just blew up the second Death Star. What are you going to do? Take it from the Scotch Trooper. When you're dancing around the Ewok village, you're going to want to be sipping Lagavulin 16. "At least for me, that's always my go-to when I feel like I've accomplished something," Ferencz reveals. "It's something that's accessible, but feels like it's a step above. You want it to be accessible, not something like Balvenie 30."

PREQUELS (I WARNED YOU)

The Phantom Menace

This one is more about what happens on the other side of the screen. Sure, *Episode I* has its fans—hell, even I saw the damn thing nine times in theaters, wanting to like it—but it really is the low point of the saga.

"You need a Laphraoiag ten-year-old cask strength to deal with watching it," says Ferencz. "There's nothing better than an Islay cask-strength whiskey. Of course, that depends on how much you can tolerate that peaty smokiness—some find it as cloying as Jar Jar Binks."

Attack of the Clones: Obi-Wan's Bar Order

Obi-Wan and Anakin are chasing bounty hunter Zam Wessell through the skyways of Coruscant. Back on the ground, Obi-Wan and his Padawan enter a bar. The Jedi Master says he's getting a drink. What does he order? A Glenfiddich highball, Ferencz confidently asserts. "I feel like he would want something that is whiskey-related, but still refreshing at the same time. For some reason, I don't see him as a neat whiskey guy at this point in his life." Foiling assassination attempts does make one thirsty, so a highball fits the bill.

Revenge of the Sith: Obi-Wan Goes into Exile

Okay, Obi-Wan is a few years older. He's also a bit battle-worn, having served as a general in the Clone Wars from beginning to end. Now, he's ready for the neat whiskey, and it's a doozy: Balvenie 30. "It's just something he's going to want to sip and savor over the next few years in isolation. It's nice, delicate and smooth, and you know he's going to savor every drop." Also, Ewan MacGregor is a Scotsman, so, there's that.

SEQUEL TRILOGY

The Force Awakens: Maz's Bar

There's a definite speakeasy vibe to Maz's joint, one that defies branding. "I just feel like it would be some people creating their own whiskey in the back, moonshining it." Be careful when you drink the stuff, though. It might cause you to have some rather violent visions that'll send you running into the woods.

The Last Jedi: Canto Bight Casino

Where the Mos Eisley Cantina is all about cheap bourbon, the ostentatious Canto Bight gambling hall is definitely a place for the high-end, special Macallan releases.

THE STANDALONES

Rogue One: Jyn and Cassian's Last Drink

Our heroes just completed their mission, but they know that they are personally doomed. The Death Star is about to use Scarif for target practice. Hopefully there's a hip flask in someone's pocket. Ferencz's pick: Glendronach 15 or something from Glenfarclas. His reasoning: "It's one of those drams for me that make me realize there's a lot of great whiskey out there that's not being overly marketed. Cassian and Jyn wouldn't be suckers to marketing."

Solo: Dryden Vos's Yacht

See also: Canto Bight casino. You get a lot of the same unsavory types of people with a lot of money to throw around—and they just want to be seen throwing it around. They just find the most expensive bottle that they can buy and do shots of it, but they wouldn't know any better. If they still use paper money, they would probably be lighting their cigars with it.

YODA GIN FIZZ

When I asked Ben Paré—bar manager at Miami's iconic Fontainebleau resort and formerly of New York's Sanctuary T—to contribute a *Star Wars*-themed drink to this collection, he was more than happy to oblige with this riff on a Ramos Gin Fizz. It's green like our favorite Jedi master.

- 2 ounces gin of choice
- 1 dash orange blossom water
- 1 large egg white
- 1 bar spoon matcha powder
- ½ ounce coconut cream
- ½ ounce fresh lemon juice
- ½ ounce fresh lime juice
- ¾ ounce simple syrup
- Seltzer (optional)
- Grated nutmeg (garnish)

Combine all ingredients in a shaker, dry shake until the egg white is fully emulsified, add ice, and shake again. Then, double strain through a fine mesh strainer into a tall Collins glass. (Top with an optional splash of seltzer for some extra froth.) Garnish with freshly grated nutmeg.

Photo Credit: Ben Paré

MOS EISLEY BY WAY OF AMSTERDAM

When most people think of drinking in Amsterdam, it usually involves a brand that rhymes with Schmeineken. But what a lot of outsiders don't realize about the Dutch capital is that it has cultivated, in just a few short years, one of the most celebrated craft cocktail scenes in all of Europe—the world even—with bars like Rosalia's Menagerie, HPS (Hiding in Plain Sight), and Tales & Spirits. The folks running Tales & Spirits have quite the geeky streak running through them and serve a mix series of pop culture-inspired cocktails, one of which is a *Star Wars* collection. Each drink in the collection features ingredients inspired by key locations in the original trilogy.

UTINNI!

Named after the notorious Jawa exclamation, Utinni! draws its inspiration from the diminutive droid dealers' (and the Mos Eisley Cantina's) home planet, Tatooine. The drink showcases spirits made from agave, which thrive in similarly dry climates. It also features a nod to Tunisia, the real-world location where George Lucas filmed the Tatooine scene. The cocktail recipe includes ras el hanout, a spice mix native to Tunisia and other North African countries.

- 1 ounce Don Julio blanco tequila
- ½ ounce Apprendiz Espadin mezcal
- ⅓ ounce Galliano Authentico
- 1 ounce orange ras el hanout elixir (see recipe below)
- ⅓ ounce simple syrup
- 2 dashes of Force tincture (see recipe below)

Stir all ingredients in a cocktail shaker and pour into a rocks glass over one large cube of ice. Garnish with lemon zest, dehydrated lime wheel, and edible violet.

For the orange ras el hanout elixir, combine 1 liter of orange juice, 10 grams of ras el hanouth, and 30 grams of citric acid.

For the Force tincture, roast and grind 10 grams of dried hibiscus, 3 grams of mace (a relative of nutmeg), 20 grams of orange peel, 5 grams of Sichuan peppercorns, 4 cardamom pods, and 5 cloves. Flash fuse in iSi with one 750 ml bottle of white rum and 100 grams of ground dark roast coffee.

TOO HOTH TO HANDLE

We move on to *The Empire Strikes Back* with "Too Hoth to Handle," which Tales & Spirits serves in a Darth Vader goblet. The bar compares the Rebel Alliance's battles against the Empire to Scotland's struggle against the English empire in the eighteenth century. Tales & Spirits also draws another parallel between the Jacobites' defeat at the Battle of Culloden to the Rebels' defeat on Hoth. Just as the Rebels went on the run after the Hoth battle, Bonnie Prince Charlie went into hiding on the Isle of Skye—where he reportedly created a special elixir that became Drambuie, a key component of this drink. (It's a stretch, I know, but the Vader head goblet is pretty cool.)

- 2 ounces Amontillado sherry
- ⅔ ounce Drambuie
- 2 dashes of Spanish bitters
- 2 dashes of Force tincture
- 2 slices of orange

Shake, strain, and serve over crushed ice in a Darth Vader goblet. Garnish with homemade maraschino cherries, mint sprig, and dehydrated orange.

Photo credit: Jeff Cioletti

BRIGHT TREE SWIZZLE

To close out the trilogy, "Bright Tree Swizzle" is a nod to *Return of the Jedi*'s central location, the forest moon of Endor. And, in honor of the Ewoks' home, the drink is full of forest botanicals. It even includes Redwood shrub (recipe below), a tribute to California's redwood forest, where the Endor scenes were filmed.

- 1 ⅓ ounces Death's Door gin
- ⅓ ounce Skinos Mastic liqueur (made from trees!)
- ⅔ ounce Smoked Redwood shrub (see recipe below)
- ½ ounce lime juice
- 2 dashes of Force tincture

Build and churn in a clay mug over crushed ice. Serve with a short straw and garnish with a cinnamon stick, seasonal berries and dehydrated lemon wheel.

For the Redwood shrub, combine 1 kilogram of mixed forest fruits, 1 bush mint, 8.5 ounces of raspberry vinegar, a little over ¾ of an ounce of Laphroaig Scotch whisky, and 1 kilogram of sugar.

THE WRETCHED HIVE

The efforts of Tales & Spirits inspired me to create a drink that draws from elements of the *Star Wars* universe. This one's a little less complicated, though boukha isn't always the easiest to find outside of major cities. If you live in a state that allows online retailers to send you alcohol through the mail, you're in luck.

This cocktail combines a spirit produced on Tatooine (sort of) with a pun. Boukha is the national spirit of Tunisia, which, of course, served as the exterior shooting location for Luke's and Anakin's home world. The "hive" is a reference to the honey in this drink. (Get it, bees?) Add a splash of dry mead to double-down on the hive. Then, throw in a lime peel garnish to give it some green, in honor of our dear, departed bounty hunter friend, Greedo. Boukha Bokobsa is the brand you're likely to find, given its international distribution. It's a fig-based distillate that's been in the founding Bokobsa family since the mid-nineteenth century.

- 2 ounces Boukha Bokobsa
- ¼ ounce dry mead
- ¼ ounce honey
- Lime wedge

Pour the boukha, mead, and honey into a cocktail shaker filled with ice. Stir vigorously. Pour into a wine glass or tulip glass. Squeeze in lime, garnish with what's left.

CHAPTER 2

THE UNITED FERMENTATION OF PLANETS

Full disclosure: I've always had a bit of an on-again, off-again relationship with *Star Trek*. I've never been a full-on Trekkie—the fact that I used that word proves it, because I believe the preferred term is "Trekker." But my earliest Star Trek memories predate those of my preferred franchise, *Star Wars*. I was five when I first visited the galaxy far, far away on its initial theatrical run in 1977. But my recollections of watching Kirk and the crew go back as early as—I think—1975. I was three years old. The show had been off the air for about six years, but the local TV station, Channel 11 WPIX-NY, broadcast reruns at around five or six every evening. I remember knowing who many of the main characters were, at least by look, if not always by name. I also had vivid memories of a vicious, albino, ape-like creature with a single horn on its head. Instead of being terrified, I always waited for that being—which, I later learned, was called a mugatu and appeared in the 1968 episode, "A Private Little War"—to make a return appearance. I was consistently disappointed.

Until I was at least seven years old, I thought the *Enterprise* crew's enemies were the "Clee-ons."

Through the years I would catch late-night episodes from time to time, and I'd see the movies either in theaters or on VHS. When *The Next Generation* started, I watched the pilot, "Encounter at Farpoint" and set my VCR for the subsequent two or three episodes—but I couldn't keep up. I'd drop in and out of the series. "Oh, Scotty's in this episode? I'm in." But by my early twenties, geekdom had become ridiculously tribal. Remember what I had said earlier about choosing a side? I chose *Star Wars* because I was, at best, a casual fan of the *Trek* series (I hadn't even seen a single episode of *Deep Space Nine* during its entire initial run) and the movies were usually hit or miss. The *Star Wars* prequel trilogy became closer and closer to becoming a reality (mid-'90s at this point) and that was giving me all sorts of warm and fuzzy feelings that I just wasn't getting from *Trek*.

But when *Star Wars* episodes I through III turned out to be… well, not so good, I realized that maybe there was a little room in my life for *Trek*. The J.J. Abrams films arrived at just the right time for that. Eventually, I binged some series episodes (including the aforementioned DS9) and realized that, in a lot of ways, *Trek* was essentially *Cheers* in space.

If there's one thing that gives me hope for the future it's that when so many genre properties get so much wrong about the role alcohol—or, at the very least, synthehol—plays in everyday life, *Star Trek* gets so much right.

DIPLOMACY

Let's jump back to the tenth episode of the original series, "The Corbomite Maneuver," which first aired on November 10, 1966. The *Enterprise* crew encounters a spinning, cube-shaped entity in deep space and they soon make contact with the imposing, bald, big-headed alien Balok, who seems anything but friendly. The alien informs them that the cube—which shadows every move the *Enterprise* makes—is just a warning. Next up: annihilation. Our fearless Federation explorers eventually end up in a standoff with Balok and, after a series of bluffs on either side, a delegation consisting of Kirk, Dr. Bones McCoy and a young, somewhat whiny Kirk-in-training named Dave Bailey (actor Anthony Call), is beamed aboard the enemy ship for a confrontation with Balok. Our heroes immediately learn that the frightening-looking being whom they thought was Balok, was, in fact a puppet. The real Balok had the body of a follicle-challenged child—seven-year-old Clint Howard, whose brother, Ron, was still trapped in Mayberry at the time and had yet to give him a cameo in just about every movie he would later direct (including 2018's *Solo: A Star Wars Story*—see, we all CAN get along). It wasn't young Clint's voice we heard, however, as he was dubbed to sound like a grown-up. (Pretty good lip-synching job for a seven-year-old, though.)

And, as it turns out, Balok is a pretty nice guy. All of his warnings and challenges were just tests to determine the *Enterprise*'s true intentions. What he really yearns for are diplomatic relations with intelligent races from across the stars (his ship was completely crew-less, so he was probably quite lonely and bored). They sealed the deal over a punch bowl full of tranya, the traditional drink of Balok's home world, poured into some rather funky glasses with wide, multi-sided stems.

The practice of forging diplomatic relations over booze is as old as booze itself. It's also about as cross-cultural as traditions come. In China, for instance, dignitaries have been known to toast with baijiu, the country's traditional spirit distilled from grain—mostly sorghum, combined with wheat, rice, barley, and whatever other cereals are available. It's known for its rather… shall we say, assertive flavor.

When President Barack Obama hosted Japanese Prime Minister Shinzō Abe at a state dinner in 2015, the President toasted the visiting leader with sake (Dassai 23 Junmai Daiginjo, to be precise). And Russians look for any excuse to say "*na zdorovie*" with a shot of vodka. Diplomatic meetings are just one of those many occasions.

If *Star Trek* is any guide, then the custom of bridging cultures (and even galaxies) by sharing a glass or two of adult beverages will survive at least a few hundred more years. After all, it did correctly predict in the '60s that we would be commanding our computers verbally, among other developments.

Tranya may have become a liquid symbol of finding common ground, but, in the real world, it's been the source of ongoing debate for more than five decades.

There's a bit of controversy over what the props team actually put in the bowl and the glassware. Clint Howard has claimed that it was grapefruit juice, which he actually hated; he had to work really hard not to betray that fact on screen. William Shatner, in his memoir, *Star Trek Memories*, remembers it being warm apricot juice with food coloring. To the naked eye, it resembled unfiltered apple juice, so there might be some truth to that.

While Anthony Call's Bailey character would never again appear on *Trek*—the *Enterprise* leaves him with Balok as an ambassador—tranya would pop up again decades later. Jadzia Dax can't get enough of it at Quark's Bar on *Deep Space Nine*.

The 2015 edition of Tiki Oasis—an annual gathering of Polynesia-philes in San Diego, (see Chapter 12) featured a symposium titled "The Interstellar Tranya: Drinking the Good Life and Beyond" hosted by Rod Roddenberry, TV producer and son of Gene Roddenberry, along with tiki expert Jonathan

Knowles and others. They presented an encore of the symposium at the Fiftieth Anniversary *Star Trek* Convention in Las Vegas a year later in an area deemed, what else, Quark's Bar.

Dueling recipes emerged from that event in a nod to the conflicting reports of the five-decades-old original drink. One was grapefruit-forward and the other, apricot-forward. Both had rum. Lots of rum. These are tiki drinks, after all.

A SENSE OF NORMALCY

The history of exploration is soaked in alcohol, and it's reassuring to find that the Federation appears to have learned from the past. Long journeys have, for centuries, involved some kind of booze. There's a popular story about the Pilgrims landing at Plymouth Rock instead of their original destination, the Jamestown colony in Virginia, because they needed to stop to make more beer. There's likely little truth to that tale which the craft beer industry likes to tell, but it is rooted, at least to some extent, in custom.

And then there are also rum and the Navy, which have been closely intertwined since about the dawn of sugarcane cultivation and distillation in the New World. They don't call higher-proof rums "navy strength" for nothing.

Whenever there is new mode of transportation, you can bet that there will be booze on board. You think folks would have been willing to get into a metal tube that would hurl them through the air at thirty-five thousand feet and speeds of more than five hundred miles per hour if the flight attendants didn't ply them with booze to help calm their nerves?

So, it's perfectly logical that the *Enterprise* and other vessels in the *Star Trek* universe have bars. You can't expect people to sign on for a five-year or continuing interstellar mission without a place to unwind, socialize and, yes, tie one on from time to time.

On the original series, we rarely got to see much of the *Enterprise*'s broader population outside of the bridge, save for a few extras walking down a corridor every now and again and the requisite Red Shirt about to meet an untimely end at some point before the closing credits rolled. The '60s version of the *Enterprise* just seemed so...lonely. You can probably thank the modest budget of a series that its network never truly believed in. It frequently got the highest ratings of its Thursday night slot (okay, there were only three networks at the time), but that didn't stop NBC from exiling it to the Friday night death slot (where it still managed to hold its own).

But, by the time *The Next Generation* was ready to embark, *Star Trek* was a bona fide phenomenon. Devoted fans kept the fire burning during the wilderness years, the decade between the airing of final original series episode "Turnabout Intruder" and the release of *Star Trek: The Motion Picture*. And the cult continued to grow during that period, thanks to nightly reruns on local TV stations. Attendance at *Trek* conventions, which began in earnest in 1972—nearly three years after the show's cancelation—grew steadily through the '70s. Star Trek Lives! gets much of the credit for being a pioneer in the convention space, but the New York City fan celebration—which ran for five consecutive years—was not the first. That honor belongs to a much smaller gathering, *Star Trek* Con in Newark, New Jersey in 1969.

The relatively brief run of *Star Trek: The Animated Series* from the fall of 1973 until the fall of 1974 also helped stoke the *Trek* revival movement.

When "Encounter at Farpoint," *The Next Generation* pilot, aired, the franchise already had four original-crew movies under its belt. The last of these, *Star Trek IV: The Voyage Home*, had been the most commercially successful of the franchise and nearly tied with *Star Trek II: The Wrath of Khan* as the most critically acclaimed of the classic crew movies; *Khan* scored 88 percent and *Voyage Home* registered 85 percent on Rotten Tomatoes. Of course, these scores were retroactive since neither Rotten Tomatoes nor the internet existed in those days. Needless to say, Paramount believed in the franchise and was willing to put some money and production value behind its new syndicated sequel series. The effects are laughable by today's standards, but they were nothing short of cutting-edge in the '80s. The production team wanted its world to be as believable as its budget and technology would allow, and that meant populating the *Enterprise*. It also meant that sometimes that population wanted to go where everybody knew their names. That watering hole had its own Sam Malone, in the form of Guinan. The fact that a very familiar face, Whoopi Goldberg, embodied the role, meant the audience would instantly bond with the barkeep, just as the crew of the *Enterprise-D* would.

Guinan's familiarity was already baked in to the series. We didn't get an episode that spent any significant amount of time introducing this new character. There was no fanfare. Her first scene didn't even have any lines (those would come later in the episode). She just *was*. Only Whoopi Goldberg could pull that off.

When it came time to launch another spinoff series—*Deep Space Nine*, (*DS9*) which debuted midway through *The Next Generation*'s sixth season—you could be damned sure there'd be a drinking establishment on the titular remote space station at the edge of a wormhole. It was such a volatile location, with peace always hanging by a thread. Booze played no small role in keeping a wide range of galactic species' worst instincts in check. And Quark, the resident publican—well, casino owner, really—was just the Ferengi for the job. Ferengi were the wheeler-dealers of the galaxy. They could be a bit sleazy, but they also knew how to defuse a heated situation. When the Cardassians withdrew from nearby Bajor, Captain Benjamin Sisko was intent on keeping Quark around as a community leader—a role played by many a bar owner throughout history and today—for a sense of continuity, of familiarity.

DS9 is the closest thing to a Western that's existed in the *Trek* franchise. There's the obvious frontier aspect to it. If Sisko was the mayor of this one-horse town on the edge of eternity, then Odo was its sheriff. Quark is very obviously its Al Swearengen (without all of the "cocksuckers"). Folks might argue that *Enterprise* was more Wild West than *DS9* because everything was so new and uncharted versus "lived-in." But I would argue that *Enterprise* was more like the age of explorers and conquistadors that predated the young America's westward migration.

ROMULAN ALE

Each beer geek has their favorites. These "addictive brews" are often rare, and brew aficionados camp out at tasting rooms or wait in lines for hours at major beer festivals to get a taste.

It doesn't seem like anyone actually likes synthehol—least among them, Captain Picard. The captain shares some of Guinan's secret stash of fluorescent green Aldebaran whiskey, which Picard himself procured for the bar. Scotty marvels at its strength, and Picard downs it in a single shot.

Captain Jean-Luc, whose family has owned a French winery for generations, knows his way around a good drink. In the episode "Family," the captain visits the Chateau Picard winery while on his post-Borg assimilation shore leave in season four, and his brother Robert—a man with a chip on his shoulder as big as his vineyard—ribs Jean-Luc about the captain's diminished ability to distinguish a 2346 vintage from a 2347 and that it's all synthehol's fault. Jean-Luc assures him that the artificial stuff heightens one's appreciation for the genuine article—and he's right.

There's no replacing tradition. The Picard family winery looks like it's straight out of the eighteenth century, not the twenty-fourth. That's because alcohol production technology—most notably oak barrel aging—was perfected hundreds of years ago and nothing has come along to improve on it. If it ain't broke, don't fix it.

Robert Picard is something of a guardian of traditions. He refuses to get a replicator—the magical food machine on the *Enterprise*—because cooking is a dying art. Jean-Luc insists such art is not lost with technology; there's just an added layer of convenience. "Life is already too convenient," Robert retorts.

Robert, if he were alive in the twenty-first century, would have made a good craft brewer. The life-is-too-convenient mantra is the raison d'etre of craft brewers, or any craft beverage maker, really. Sure, massive industrial production and the modern

supply chain made beer more convenient in the twentieth
century, but the beverage lost its soul. Craft brewers restored
the soul by championing quality and flavor over convenience.
Hopefully that value system persists well into the twenty-fourth
century, as it does with Robert. Hopefully it won't die with him
when he and his son burn to death (off-screen) years later in *Star
Trek: Generations*.

WHERE NO MALT HAS
GONE BEFORE

For a TV series and movie franchise (and merchandising
bonanza) as venerable as *Star Trek*, it's kind of amazing that it
took nearly five decades for there to be an officially licensed
beer line. A Canadian company—in Calgary, Alberta, to be
precise—that goes by the name Federation of Beer, negotiated
the license with CBS Television to bring these brews into our
century. I remember running into a bunch of people dressed as
Klingons at the 2014 Nightclub & Bar Show in Vegas when the
company was promoting the partnership. Federation of Beer
doesn't actually brew the beers; nor would they be considered a
contract brewer in the traditional sense.

They've teamed with a number of US- and Canada-based
breweries to produce an ongoing series of limited-edition *Star
Trek* beers. But Federation of Brewing acts more as a silent
partner in the enterprise (sorry, had to), as the brewers maintain
their own branding on the releases. Clifton Park, New York's
Shmaltz Brewing Co. (best known for its He'Brew line) has
marketed such beers as Golden Anniversary Ale: The Trouble
with Tribbles, commemorating the fiftieth anniversary of the *Star
Trek* franchise in 2016; Symbiosis, a hoppy wheat celebrating

the thirtieth anniversary of *Star Trek: The Next Generation* the following year; Klingon Imperial Porter and Deep Space Nine Profit Motive, a generously hopped golden ale inspired by Quark's Bar, released in 2018 to coincide with *Deep Space Nine*'s twenty-fifth anniversary.

Halifax, Nova Scotia-based Garrison Brewing has produced Klingon Warnog Roggen Dunkel, a dark rye, and Red Shirt Ale, an amber brew that's a nod to the ill-fated *Enterprise* crewmembers who wear their crimson attire like a target on their backs.

BALOK'S BEST OF BOTH WORLDS: NON-TRADITIONAL TRANYA

As mentioned earlier, there's been a bit of controversy about the contents of the prop tranya back in 1966—Clint Howard swears it was grapefruit juice while William Shatner insists that it was apricot juice. Since tranya was a symbol of diplomacy and interplanetary understanding, my version has an equal amount of both. Since it's sort of tiki-ish, I wanted it to be rum-based—particularly rhum agricole. I also wanted to include something distilled from Iowa grain, as a nod to everyone's favorite Iowan, a man by the name of James Tiberius Kirk. That's where the Iowa unaged corn or rye whiskey (a.k.a. moonshine, but it's legal) comes in.

- 2 ounces white rhum agricole (Rhum Clément and Rhum Barbancourt are accessible options)
- 1 ounce Iowa white dog/moonshine/unaged corn whiskey (Country Gal Moonshine from Iowa Distilling Co., Two Jay's Iowa Corn Whiskey from Broadbent Distillery, River Baron Artisan Spirit from Mississippi River Distilling Co., and Iowa Legendary White Rye are some good examples; if you can't find anything from Iowa, any unaged whiskey will do)
- 2 ounces grapefruit juice
- 2 ounces apricot juice
- 2 dashes orange bitters

Pour all ingredients in a shaker full of ice. Stir well. Strain and serve up in a stemless Cosmo glass because it most closely resembles the glassware in which Balok served tranya to his guests. (If you don't have this, a rocks glass is fine.) If you really want to go full Balok, scale it up and serve it out of a punch bowl.

VULCAN-O

The good folks at Beeline Creative, the makers of Geeki Tikis cocktail mugs, teamed up with noted tropical drinks and tiki bar expert, personality, and consultant Blair Reynolds on this concoction—a twist on the classic Leilani Volcano. Reynolds also markets his own line of drinks syrups called B.G. Reynolds, one of which is a component of this drink. Reynolds created it specifically for Geeki Tikis' Spock mug, but any tiki vessel or tall glass will suffice.

- 1 ounce blue curaçao
- ½ ounce coconut rum
- 2 ounces guava nectar
- 1 ounce pineapple juice
- ¾ ounces fresh lime juice
- ½ ounce B.G. Reynolds Lush Grenadine (or equivalent)
- Mint sprig (garnish)
- Lime wheel (garnish)

Shake the first five ingredients with crushed ice and pour into the mug. Top with crushed ice, float the grenadine, and garnish with a mint sprig and lime wheel.

The Vulcan-O (in Geeki Tikis Spock mug). Photo credit: Perfect Drink®
(Special thanks to Beeline Creative)

POLICE
POLICE TELEPHONE
FREE
FOR USE OF
PUBLIC
ADVICE & ASSISTANCE
OBTAINABLE IMMEDIATELY
OFFICER & CARS
RESPOND TO ALL CALLS
PULL TO OPEN

CHAPTER 3
A DOCTOR WALKS INTO A PUB...

The Doctor, and all of his (and now her) incarnations, is a thousands of years old Time Lord from the planet Gallifrey who has the ability to regenerate into a new form, taking on an entirely new face, body and—as glass-TARDIS-ceiling smasher Jodie Whittaker has once and for all proven—gender. But what's most appealing to me is not that the Doctor is a time-traveling alien, but that at heart he is incredibly British. (That doesn't just mean English. The character has been played by no fewer than three Scotsmen thus far). The television show, *Doctor Who*, made its debut in 1963, and since then has been a show by Brits for Brits, which meant the hero had to be somewhat relatable for the target audience. That means, over the course of its nearly six-decade history—we won't talk about the wasteland years when the show didn't air—the longest-running sci-fi series in history lacked the puritanical tendencies of its counterparts across the pond when it came to social drinking.

Of course, when you're dealing with a character who has had thirteen different personalities—fourteen when you count John Hurt's War Doctor—you're likely to get a plethora of favorite tipples and approaches to drinking.

The obvious example is the third Doctor (Jon Pertwee). The producers at the time seemed intent on harnessing some of the 007 mojo that had swept Britain (and the world) over the prior decade. Pertwee's tenure officially began in January 1970 and

Doctor number three was a man of action with a penchant for gadgets. Pertwee's Doctor spent most of his first three seasons stuck on Earth, which made it easier to sell the more Bond-ian elements, down to both iconic British characters' automotive fixation. Instead of an Aston Martin, though, the Doctor drove "Bessie," a yellow, vintage, Edwardian-era roadster.

In the four-part serial, "The Three Doctors"—the first story in which the Doctor teams with his former selves—the first Doctor (played by William Hartnell), in one of his very few scenes, dubs his two future incarnations "a dandy and a clown." The third Doctor is the former, a trait he shares in some respects with James Bond. Doctor number one was referring to the third Doctor's manner of dress: the velvet jacket, the frilly shirt, the black dress pants, and cape with purple lining. He'd often wear a bow tie as well.

Bond was known for his impeccable style as well, from the signature tux to the tailored suits. But where the iconic MI6 agent's and the third Doctor's high-class tastes really overlapped was in their respective eating and drinking habits. Pertwee's version of the Time Lord and 007 both fancied themselves connoisseurs. (See Chapter 9 for in-depth details on the latter's habits.)

In the classic 1972 story, "The Day of the Daleks," the Doctor and companion Jo Grant indulge in some of the contents of diplomat Sir Reginald Styles's wine cellar while they're house-sitting after an assassination attempt by guerrillas from two hundred years in the future. When the Doctor is done rhapsodizing about the quality of gorgonzola cheese that Styles keeps on hand, he dives into a glass of red wine. And, not only does he drink it, he offers his own Doctor-ish tasting notes: "a most good-humored wine—a touch sardonic, perhaps, but not

cynical. Yes, a most civilized wine, one after my own heart."
(The description could very well apply to James Bond, as well,
though I would say 007 has a touch more cynicism.) It's enough
for Jo to observe that the Doctor is "carrying on like a one-man
food and wine society."

For all intents and purposes, Pertwee's third Doctor is the first
real drinker among the early incarnations. Doctor number one
flat-out lied two times when offered a drink in the Old West—
Tombstone, to be exact, of OK Corral fame in the 1966 story
"The Gunfighters." The Doctor (with companions Steven and
Dodo) arrived in 1881 Arizona Territory with a monster of a
toothache. Of course, Tombstone was home to a very famous
dentist, one Doc "I'm Your Huckleberry" Holliday. When the first
Doctor enlisted Holliday's services, the Time Lord was hoping
for an anesthetic. This being a good quarter century before the
invention of novocaine, all that the dentist and gunslinger had
to offer was a slug of "rattlesnake oil" (most likely whiskey) but
Doctor number one was adamant about not letting booze touch
his time-traveling lips.

Later in the same serial, he reiterated his dry commitment
when offered a drink in a saloon, noting that he'd be fine with
just a glass of milk. (It's no wonder "The Gunfighters" was
long regarded as the worst story in the history of the long-
running series.)

A year earlier—well, technically eight hundred and fifteen years
earlier in the historical timeline—the Doctor rather enjoyed
drinking mead at the Battle of Hastings in the serial, "The Time
Meddler." The first Doctor didn't abstain when offered Madeira
in "The Smugglers," but he did turn down brandy, which
leads me to believe that it's not so much alcohol that Hartnell's

incarnation detests, but distilled spirits (despite the fact that Madeira is often fortified with brandy).

I wouldn't be surprised if the Doctor's anti-drinking stance came from Hartnell himself. He always viewed *Doctor Who* as a children's show rather than a "family" show. There's a distinction. Adults are bored out of their skulls watching children's shows. But they enjoy family shows as much as their kids do, if not more so. The actor often was reportedly at odds with the production team any time the show got too scary for the kiddies. (Once those genies known as the Daleks were out of their bottles, there was no going back.) Hartnell's declining health—which often manifested on-screen with botched lines—has been put forth as the primary reason the actor vacated the role, but the narrative direction of the series also played at least some small part in his departure.

Of course, when a Doctor regenerates, their personality changes considerably. Hartnell's Doctor was a crotchety old bastard and it was probably best that we never got to see him inebriated. On the other hand, it may have made him lighten up a bit.

All future incarnations, save for number six and number twelve, were far less cranky than number one. Regeneration mellowed the Doctor considerably. Doctor number nine, played by actor Christopher Eccleston, might seem to be a rough-around-the-edges Manchester football hooligan on the outside, but he does seem to share his third incarnation's penchant for elegant adult beverages. In "World War III," the second of the two-part Slitheen invasion story in the first season of the freshly rebooted series, the Doctor, his companion Rose Tyler, and future Prime Minster Harriet Jones pour themselves glasses of what looks like either port, sherry, or brandy (hi-def was barely a thing when that episode came out) from a decanter sitting at the center of a conference table at 10 Downing Street. Moments earlier, the Doctor threatened to ignite the booze with his sonic screwdriver and use it as a weapon against the Slitheen. Once they were safe inside the fortified walls of the British government's situation room—and just after they listened on the phone to Jackie Tyler (Rose's mother) and Mickey Smith (Rose's beau) blow up a Slitheen in the kitchen—the trio took a moment for a celebratory toast.

It was quite a familiar setting for the Doctor. Hours earlier, in the preceding episode, "Aliens of London," number nine noted that a former Prime Minister drank him under the table. (Is the Doctor a lightweight?)

Once the Doctor and crew defeated the Slitheen, Jackie was eager to have over for tea the man who whisked her daughter across galaxies and millennia. Jackie noted that she had a bottle of Amaretto on hand and asked whether the Doctor was a drinker. Rose answered in the affirmative. I'm pretty sure the conference room wasn't the first time she saw him imbibe.

We've even seen the Doctor drunk. In the episode with the tenth Doctor, "The Girl in the Fireplace," the Time Lord staggers home from a soiree in eighteenth century Paris and claims to have accidentally invented the banana daiquiri hundreds of years too early. And this is why number ten remains my favorite.

A few years later, the eleventh Doctor gets a call from a nursing home, notifying him that Brigadier Lethbridge-Stewart has passed away. The character never made a proper reappearance on the revived series—his last on-screen appearance was in the 1989 story, "Battlefield"—though he did guest star on the *Doctor Who* spinoff, *The Sarah Jane Adventures.*

The nurse on the other end of the line told the Doctor that the Brigadier "always made us pour an extra brandy in case you came 'round one of these days." (His actor, Nicholas Courtney, was quite the bon vivant. In 2001, I interviewed him for my documentary, *Chronotrip*, and I made sure to include a shot of his handler bringing him a drink from the hotel bar once the interview was done).

We do learn in one of the Doctor's much later incarnations—the unapologetically Scottish one—that the Time Lord hides a bottle or two of booze behind one of the "round things" in the TARDIS.

In Peter Capaldi's final outing, "Twice Upon a Time," we get one of the strangest multi-Doctor episodes to date. Number twelve, in the prolonged throes of regeneration, bumps into number one (William Hartnell), also in the throes of his own prolonged regeneration into Patrick Troughton. Wait, you say. Didn't William Hartnell die in 1975? And didn't Richard Hurndall, who stepped in for Hartnell for "The Five Doctors" in 1983, pass away less than a year after that?

Then-showrunner Steven Moffat's solution to that conundrum was a genius move. He rehired David Bradley (best known as Argus Filch in the *Harry Potter* flicks and Walder Frey on *Game of Thrones*), who had played William Hartnell four years earlier in *An Adventure in Time & Space*, the docudrama that chronicled the creation and early years of *Doctor Who*. (So, I would argue that Bradley has an even greater claim to the role than Hurndall did).

There's a scene when Doctors one and twelve are both inside the TARDIS (in this case, the twelfth Doctor's TARDIS) with an English World War I army captain (Mark Gatiss, who, fun fact, actually wrote *An Adventure in Time and Space*). Naturally, any early-twentieth-century human is going to completely freak out when he encounters such a marvel of trans-dimensional engineering, so the captain started to feel a little faint and dizzy. Recognizing that the soldier was in shock, Doctor number one told number twelve to fetch the man some brandy. "Do you have any?" number one asks. "I had some…somewhere." Aha! So you DO touch alcohol, number one. Quite the contradiction!

Hiding behind the panel was a bottle of Aldebaran brandy, a decanter and a couple of glasses. It's not the first time this secret stash appeared. Exactly two years earlier (in Earth time), River Song revealed the little Aldebaran brandy bar when she boarded the TARDIS and didn't yet recognize number twelve as the Doctor. I actually thought she was the one who had put it there until David Bradley's number one acknowledged that he usually kept some around. I'm pretty sure River and number one never crossed paths, but who can be entirely sure? Spoilers!

If that name sounds familiar, it's because it's appeared multiple times in science fiction, as well as science fact. And it often has something to do with booze (on the fiction side, that is). In *Star Trek: The Next Generation*, for instance, Guinan always had a stash of Aldebaran whiskey, and the green-hued spirit popped up on *Deep Space Nine*, as well. *Hitchhiker's Guide to the Galaxy* fans—who, understandably, overlap a great deal with Whovians—will recognize it as the place where, according to Milliways (the restaurant at the end of the universe) emcee Max Quordlepleen, fine liqueurs are made.

Aldebaran folks obviously are quite prolific distillers, so how do we get there?

You're in luck because Aldebaran, also known as Alpha Tau, is actually a real place. Aldebaran is a star about sixty-five light-years from our solar system. That means, all that you need to do to get there is board a vessel that travels at the speed of light and keep yourself entertained for six and a half decades until you get there. You're probably going to want to stay there because that whole relativity thing means earth likely won't even remotely resemble what it was before you embarked on the voyage.

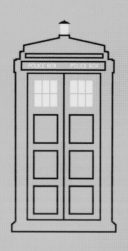

NUMBER FIVE'S G&T (GIN AND TARDIS)

I generally am not that big a fan of brightly colored drinks, especially those that require certain unnatural additives to achieve their dayglow hues. However, that presents a bit of a conundrum when I want to make something that's police-box blue to sip during episodes of *Doctor Who*. The easy solution is to start with a liqueur-like blue curaçao and reverse engineer it from there. But I don't want easy solutions, nor am I usually in the mood for anything with blue curaçao. (Certain tiki drinks get a pass, since they're rooted in kitsch.) Luckily, there's been a small wave of tinted gins produced in recent years with colors that don't detract from all of the botanical goodness in gin. And, with a series so inextricably linked with England, is there a more appropriate spirit than London No. 1 Blue Gin? It is an ideal choice for obvious reasons, as long as you're okay with the fact that it's a couple shades lighter than the broken-chameleon-circuit exterior of the TARDIS. That's why you're not going to want to go too heavy on the tonic. What makes this the "Number Five" is the celery—the fifth Doctor's oddest fashion accessory.

- 2 parts London No. 1 Blue Gin
- 1 part tonic (don't skimp. Try something good like Fever-Tree or Bermondsey Tonic. Both are from London, so they really sell the police box connection. To make the blue hue even deeper, use any of the new high-end tinted tonics coming on the market, like Fitch & Leedes Blue Tonic)
- Three splashes of Fee Brothers Celery Cocktail Bitters
- Celery (garnish)

- Fill a tall (preferably box-like) glass with ice. Pour in the gin and then the tonic. Splash in the celery bitters and stir well. Garnish with a stalk of celery. When finished, eat the celery. Don't be tempted to attach it to your lapel.

TAR-TINI

Okay maybe you're more of a martini person. The blue gin lends itself to that. It just won't be in a tall, TARDIS-like glass.

- 3 ounces London No. 1 Blue Gin or Empress 1908 Indigo Gin
- ½ ounce dry vermouth
- 2–3 dashes of Fee Brothers Celery Cocktail Bitters
- Small celery stick (garnish)

Pour the first three ingredients into a cocktail shaker or mixing glass with plenty of ice. Stir well (DO. NOT. SHAKE.) and strain into a martini glass. Garnish with a small celery stick. (Make sure it's not too long, otherwise, things will get a little clumsy.)

CHAPTER 4
SIPPING WHILE SUPER

Assemble! Photo Credit: © Beeline Creative

Let's address the caped elephant in the room: comic book characters can't seem to hold their liquor. For the purposes of this section, "comic book characters" means both their personas on the page and on the screen. So, I'm going to hopscotch between the two a bit.

Remember in the movie, *Superman III*, when everyone's favorite Kryptonian refugee became his misanthropic alter ego? I know, most of us are trying to block out any memory of that celluloid travesty, but just humor me for a moment. Before his "good side" inexplicably splits off from him in the form of Clark Kent (I'm pretty sure the earth's sun doesn't really give Kal-El that power; they were just making it up as they went along), we find our blue-tighted hero pounding shots in a dive bar. "Oh no!" we all gasp as we collectively clutch our pearls. "Superman doesn't DRINK! He must really be BAD!" I guess we'd all pretty much forgotten that he popped the cork on a bottle of champagne just prior to bedding Lois Lane for the first time in the previous film.

Audiences for superhero movies and their comic book source material are largely full of impressionable minors. Writers and studios are supposed to be After-School-Specialing them away from booze and drugs and all that, but part of the reason for alcohol abuse in this country—particularly where underage drinking is concerned—is that booze is too often portrayed as "evil" in pop culture. So when Superman goes on a bender after his brain is warped by some bizarre space rock, everyone's "Just Say No" meter kicks in.

But enough about DC/Warner Brothers. The Marvel realm has had its own uneasy relationship with alcohol. Does the name Tony Stark ring a bell?

Back in 1979, nearly three decades before Robert Downey Jr. donned the red and gold armor for the first time (and a good decade or so before the first of Downey's own substance-abuse-related run-ins with the law), Marvel ran a story arc in *The Invincible Iron Man* series titled "Demon in a Bottle." Over the course of the nine-issue run, the mega-rich playboy genius who likes to dress up in a metal suit from time to time struggled with the very serious disease of alcoholism. Though, in those days, mega-rich didn't mean billionaire, as we would describe Stark today. It is quite quaint to look back and see Stark referred to as a millionaire in the '70s.

The story line works because the writers plant seeds throughout the nine-issue run without getting too preachy. There's a lot going on plot-wise and Tony's boozing begins as a subtler subplot. We catch up with Mr. Stark—complete with '70s haircut and suit—on board a commercial airliner flying across the ocean. (Why one of the richest people in the world is flying commercial is beyond me, but I never worked at Marvel, so I'll just shut up now.) On his tray table, there are three very conspicuous bottles of gin, and they are not the 50-ml bottles you'd normally find on a plane. These bottles are about three times that size. Before he even utters a word, we know that for each bottle of gin, he is a sheet to the wind. The flight attendant asks him if he wants a magazine, but he tells her he wants another martini. She's reluctant because he's already had more than his fair share. He implores her with some sexist verbiage about her "beautiful brown eyes"—very 1970s, right?—and then adds, in his thought bubble, "After all, I'm drinking for two men." Tony Stark is still Iron Man's secret identity at this point, though it's laughable that Iron Man works as Stark's "bodyguard." Talk about insulting people's intelligence!

The PSA-style moment comes to an abrupt end when a Sherman tank hurtles toward the plane (at thirty thousand feet, mind you) and breaks off its wing. Stark is forced to battle gravity and head to the lavatory so he can put on his "work clothes" and save the day.

Over the course of the next eight issues, we get an evil oil company scheme on a remote island, an encounter with Sub-Mariner, a flashback to Iron Man's origin story in Vietnam, a few appearances by some of the other A-list Avengers, and even a Mayor Ed Koch cameo. And the alcoholism-related conflict continues to escalate. Beyond the usual comic-booky elements, it's a remarkably adult story in theme and in execution—a rarity for the 1970s when most of the world still wasn't taking comics seriously.

There's even a clever allegory for Tony's boozing interspersed with its more literal representation. The villains figure out a way to remotely manipulate Iron Man's armor against his will and force him to assassinate the UN ambassador from the fictional country of Carnelia. Iron Man loses control, just as Tony's drinking is making him lose control. He's ultimately exonerated, but people, especially kids, are still scared of him; this symbolizes the scars and sometimes irreparable harm that alcoholism causes among one's loved ones.

There's a series of less metaphoric signs of addiction: Tony yells at and condescends to his butler, Jarvis (the human one), who resigns. And that even causes Tony to lose control of his own company, Stark International. Tony's alcohol-induced short fuse makes Jarvis skittish about asking his boss for a salary advance to cover his mother's surgery. Jarvis takes the path of least resistance and hits up a rather shady bank for the loan. Some predatory practices hidden in the loan agreement force Jarvis to give up his collateral—two shares of Stark International, all that stands between SHIELD and the majority stake it was eyeing. SHIELD swoops in, rendering Stark a minority stakeholder of the corporation that bears his name.

He unsuccessfully tries to run away from himself and his problems by giving up Tony Stark and becoming Iron Man full time. It doesn't work. Every time Iron Man tries to help, he screws up. He botches the rescue of a derailed tanker full of chlorine gas by dropping it. Before he drops it, evacuation isn't necessary. Now, because he caused the gas to leak out, evacuation is critical.

Tony ultimately reaches out to Bethany Cabe for help, even though he also had been alienating her with his temper and erratic behavior. We learn that her late husband was a pill addict who drove his car off a bridge to his death, so she knows all about addiction.

Amidst all of this super-seriousness, there is some unintended humor. When Tony drinks at his "favorite Forest Hills nightclub," the narrator says, "even one-hundred-year-old brandy can't seem to lighten his burden." So, he switches to Cognac. Cognac is a type of brandy, damn it!

There is also some faux product placement. The whiskey of choice in Marvel-land is Jack Powers Old No. 7 Kentucky Whiskey. It's very obviously supposed to be Jack Daniel's—Tennessee whiskey, not Kentucky whiskey—because of the near-identical trade dress, though, at another point we get a shout out to a very real gin brand: Gilbey's.

I also had to laugh when Tony drank glass after glass of whiskey sours—if for no other reason than it gave me flashbacks to college.

BOOZY AND BADASS

In other, more modern (and adult-oriented) comics, alcohol's role becomes a bit more complex. The world becomes a little less black and white. Booze still plays the role of monkey-on-the-back in some instances, but in others it becomes a symbol of devil-may-care toughness and badassery. Both elements often exist in the same characters.

Jessica Jones tends to have one foot in each world: the disease and the badass badge of honor. Early in the very first issue of the comic *Alias*, we find Jessica lying unconscious with her head on a bar (Luke Cage's, of course) with a glass of whiskey next to her, not likely the first she's had that day—I'm guessing she was on her eighth at that point. Then again, she has superpowers and probably has a much higher tolerance than most of us.

In season one of the Netflix streaming series, her whiskey-chugging is a means of asserting her strength, essentially saying, "I can throw down with the best of them, male or female." It reminded me a great deal of the scene in *Raiders of the Lost Ark* when we first meet Marion. You know, the one where she handily defeats all male opponents in a hardcore drinking contest. (Frankly, Marion's accomplishment is a bit more impressive because she lacks Jessica's superpowers.) Jessica, in season one, utters one of the best lines summing up exactly who she is and why the former superhero became a private investigator: "I'm just trying to make a living. You know, booze costs money."

By season two, as her post-Kilgrave PTSD aggressively becomes all-consuming, her imbibing becomes a lot more tragic. Naturally, she self-medicates with booze. Tincup Whiskey, produced by Stranahan's in Colorado, makes more than a few appearances, which is surprising since there are far cheaper options. Tincup's not Single Malt Scotch expensive, but you're likely to pay at least thirty-five dollars for a 750-ml bottle.

It's not exactly a product placement for Tincup, because we never see a brand name. Then again, it doesn't actually have a label; the name is embossed on the glass. However, the hexagonal bottle shape is so damn recognizable.

On a second viewing, one can recognize a lot more bottles on her apartment and office shelves, as well. And those brands, if nothing else, underline just how complicated a human being— well, super-human being—Jessica Jones really is. She keeps a bottle of Bulleit bourbon as her "everyday" whiskey. It's as sippable as it is mixable and you can usually get your hands on a 750-ml bottle for under thirty dollars. It's strategically located on her middle shelf—exactly where it should be. If you press pause to see what she is keeping above that, sure enough, it is literally a top-shelf product: Van Brunt Stillhouse Whiskey, which usually retails for more than sixty dollars a bottle. It's produced in Red Hook, Brooklyn, just across the East River from Jess's Manhattan home turf. Isn't it great that she's keeping it local?

She also keeps the cheapest of the cheap for when she really wants to punish—or, in some cases heal—herself. One of the best season two moments occurs when Jessica's trying to disinfect a wound on her shoulder with bourbon. Her (spoiler alert!) long-believed-dead mother, Alisa, demands that she let her do it so she doesn't waste good booze. "It's bottom shelf," Jessica snaps back. It's thrilling to see that Jessica has most of the major price tiers covered.

All of this shows us that, on some level, she really would like to be a moderate drinker—a connoisseur even. If she were only interested in buying herself a one-way ticket to oblivion, she'd likely only ever buy the low-end stuff. Why waste money on the good stuff if you have no plans to enjoy or remember the experience of savoring it? Jessica's got layers, man!

Ms. Jones's drinking habits may be excessive and she's probably a (barely) functioning alcoholic. However, it makes her much more human—despite her super-human strength—and therefore, much more relatable. We don't just see her pounding shot after shot or drinking straight from the bottle. We see the effects of that behavior. She's passed out. She gets belligerent and kicked out of bars. She experiences oppressive hangovers just like the rest of us. (You know, when you are ultra-sensitive to sunlight and choose to leave sunglasses on all day, inside and out?) There's never any doubt that Jessica's self-destructive behavior takes its toll, and I really hope she stops soon. Nevertheless, she's got an eye for decent whiskey!

A HELL OF A GOOD TIME

Leave it to Dark Horse Comics to be the publisher that shows us the lighter side of drinking. I'm talking, of course, about the brainchild of Mike Mignola, Hellboy. Our tall, crimson-colored hero with the sawed-off satanic horns may be cranky on his best days, but he knows how to have a good time. And while, yes, there's an element of that "I'm a boozy badass" thing that pervades more grown-up comics, Hellboy still knows how to unwind and have a good time without going overboard (usually).

He also knows how to be the good-natured devil on the shoulder of his pal, Abe Sapien, when he wants the amphibious do-gooder to loosen up and share a six-pack of Tecate with him after a long, stressful day. Hellboy kept a whole locker full of the Mexican brand for his paranormal happy hours in the film *Hellboy II: The Golden Army*. Not only do Hellboy and Abe drink together, they sing along to Barry Manilow's "Can't Smile Without You." (Abe's pining for Princess Nuala. Long story.)

In the comics, Hellboy has had some rather curious drinking buddies. At the beginning of the two-issue story, "The Island," we catch up with Hellboy aboard a wrecked ship on a remote island, enjoying seemingly flaming tankards full of rum with what appears to be a British naval crew from the time of the Napoleonic Wars, and, true-to-form, there's a sing-along. This time it's an old sailing song, "The Mermaid." Their revelry is interrupted by a knock on the door. Hellboy gets up to check it out and, when he turns around, the crew members are revealed to be inanimate skeletons, having likely languished in that spot for two-hundred years.

The knock on the door came from a mysterious woman in a cape and the moment produces what is, perhaps, one of the most repeated lines among fans of the comic book series: "Don't mess with me, lady. I've been drinking with skeletons." I use that line any chance I get, especially at Halloween parties.

THE BOY IN THE BOTTLE

It's likely that Hellboy's belligerent, bon vivant persona made him ripe for all sorts of potable brand tie-ins. In 2015, Dark Horse Comics collaborated with the Newport, Oregon craft brewery Rogue Ales on the release of Right Hand of Doom Red Ale, featuring our favorite demon-spawn on the label. It was no accident that the team chose 2015 as the launch year. The Hellboy comic was born in 1994, so it reached legal drinking age in 2015.

A year later, Hellboy got his own wine when Dark Horse joined forces with Stoller Family Estate to unveil Hellboy Reserve Pinot Noir, a 2011 reserve red which, like the beer sports Mignola's unmistakable artwork, appealed to millennial drinkers who are done with pretensions of the wine world of yesteryear.

Truly proving that there's something for everyone, two years after Hellboy's first official brew and less than a year after his inaugural wine, his first official spirit was released. This time,

Dark Horse teamed up with Prestige Imports and Tennessee-based XXX Distillery (yep, that's its real name) to release Hellboy Hell Water Cinnamon Whiskey, a 66.6 proof (33.3 percent ABV) with a corn distillate base and natural cinnamon flavor.

Now that sounds like one *hell* of a party.

THE BLACK WIDOW

This is another cocktail from Fontainebleau's Ben Paré, inspired by Natasha Romanoff/Romanova, the Russian-born Avenger extraordinaire and Scarlett Johansson's most steady paycheck. It's black like Natasha's leather suit, bittersweet, dark, and includes ginger beer (because Romanova's a ginger). Could it be any more on the nose?

- 1½ ounces Stolichnaya vodka
- ¾ ounce Fernet Branca (or similar digestif or amaro)
- ½ bar spoon of activated charcoal powder
- 5 ounces of ginger beer
- ½ ounce lime juice

Combine all ingredients in a tall Collins glass. Swizzle, top with ice, and serve.

HULK SMASH

In the screen version of *The Avengers*, there's been a bit of steamy sexual tension between Ms. Romanova and one Dr. Bruce Banner. So, what better companion for the Black Widow than the Hulk Smash? This mean, green riff on a vodka smash is another Ben Paré creation.

- 1 ½ ounce citrus vodka
- 1 ounce Midori
- ¾ ounce lemon juice
- ½ ounce simple syrup
- 1 handful fresh mint (garnish)

Combine the first four ingredients in a shaking tin. Shake vigorously with ice. Strain over fresh crushed ice and garnish with a mint sprig.

CHAPTER 5

"THAT'S WHAT I DO, I DRINK AND I KNOW THINGS"

It is amazing that kings clash and swords storm in Westeros when so many of its inhabitants in positions of power seemed to be hammered all the time. It's really hard to plan wars when you're constantly nursing a hangover. And it's astonishing that only a few of the Westerosi elite have given up drinking all together when so many of them are getting poisoned or narrowly averting ingesting something deadly. There are two major occurrences just in the first book, *A Game of Thrones*, and in the inaugural season of the HBO adaptation that either threaten to, or succeed in, altering the course of history in (and beyond) the Seven Kingdoms.

I'm going to go ahead and say it: Robert Baratheon was a shitty king with, at best, a tenuous claim to the Iron Throne. Sure, the King Robert we meet seems light-years removed from the young warrior, who, seventeen years prior led a successful rebellion against Mad King Aerys Targaryen II. He's a much lazier, more bloated, and more gluttonous version of himself, much in the same way that another king, '70s Elvis, was a pale shadow of his pelvis-swiveling, 1950s self. If television and guns existed in Westeros, you could bet that more than a few of Robert's TVs would have met the business end of a revolver. Where Mr. Presley had his prescription painkillers, Robert Baratheon had his wine. And both were the undoing of their respective users.

King Robert had a very hearty appetite for wine. Rarely was his goblet empty. Whether he was watching a jousting tournament or hunting, he was always in his cups. That latter activity was, literally, the death of him. Cersei has her cousin/sidepiece Lancel fill the King's drinking pouch with a fortified version of Robert's favorite sour red wine, three times as potent as his usual tipple. It makes the king loopy and stupid enough to be vulnerable to a boar attack. What is supposed to be the king's prey during a hunt becomes his predator.

Robert's favorite wine was likely a Dornish red, as the southernmost Westerosi kingdom of Dorne is known for its crimson-hued sours. The variety he consumes on his fateful wild pig hunting trip is the Dornish strongwine, a much higher in ABV, fuller bodied, and more bloodlike riff on the flagship red. (Interestingly, another Dornish liquid—this time a full-on poison—is what does in Cersei's daughter, Myrcella, in the TV version. What goes around, comes around, I guess.)

If fish or chicken is on the menu, you're likely going to be drinking Arbor Gold, the closest thing to white wine that's made in Westeros. The Arbor is a smallish island off the southwestern coast of the fictional country (a country that vaguely resembles a third grader's attempted rendering of Great Britain). The Arbor does make its fair share of reds, as well, but Dorne is far better known for them. I like to think of The Arbor as something along the lines of New Zealand's North Island. The climate is probably fairly similar and Kiwi winemakers are best known for their Sauvignon Blanc. However, Arbor Gold is of a considerably lower quality than those world-class varietals, if we take Tyrion Lannister at his word. He once described an even less desirable wine as "closer to piss than Arbor Gold."

Despite the fact that the world that George R.R. Martin created has the wonkiest of climates—multiyear winters, anyone?—his famously otherworldly attention to detail carries over to booze climates. The development of traditional beer cultures versus wine cultures was very much about geography. If you look at a map of Europe (of which the Ice and Fire world is very clearly an alternate-universe version), you pretty much can draw a horizontal line down the middle and determine which areas are wine producers and which are brewing beer. Those regions are often referred to as the wine and beer belts. The more southerly regions were conducive to grape growing and that's why countries like Spain, France, Italy, Greece, and Croatia developed robust winemaking traditions. The United Kingdom, Ireland, Germany, Belgium, and the Czech Republic became synonymous with beer because barley is resilient in less temperate climates. Naturally, there's some crossover. Germany's a big country with plenty of microclimates, and it has been responsible for quite a few distinctive wines. The same goes for Austria. The flip side is true for France. A sliver of the French north is particularly famous for its bières *de garde*.

There is also the vodka belt—Poland, Russia, and the Nordic countries—but distillation emerged much later than simple fermentation. These countries were fermenting whatever they could get their hands on. For example, kvass, an Eastern European beverage, is fermented from rye bread (though the alcohol content has been considerably lower than that of beer).

The alcohol belts of Westeros are very similar to those of Europe. The southern kingdoms, generally, supply the wine, while the northern ones crank out the beer. Essos, the vast strip of land on the eastern side of the Narrow Sea, is known mostly for its wines as well. Its northernmost latitude roughly corresponds with the top edge of the southern half of Westeros, so, for the most part, grapes hold up rather well. Slaver's Bay, Lys, Volantis, Andalos, Pentos, and Astapor are all known for wines of widely variable character.

And then there's the so-called wine of courage, which appears to be somewhere between an aromatized wine (like vermouth) and an herbal liqueur. It contains a mostly secret mixture of herbs and roots and is the typical drink of the Unsullied, the Astapori army of enslaved eunuchs whose testicles and penises are removed at a young age so they're not distracted from their singular purpose in life—warfare—by anything as silly as sexuality (though it never stopped the most notable Unsullied, Grey Worm, from having a crush on Missandei, and even they figured out a way to do the deed). They drink the wine of courage to make themselves indifferent to pain—and more disciplined, obedient, and effective killing machines.

THE NORTH REMEMBERS (VERY LITTLE BECAUSE BEER)

Northern Westeros and the frosty lands beyond the Wall are essentially Northern Europe and, therefore, are in the Ice and Fire universe's equivalent of the beer belt. So, in Winterfell, you'd get the sort of dark ales for which northern English cities have become famous. And, for the most part—at least on the TV series—you get the accents to match.

Sean Bean grew up in Sheffield and his trademark is his Yorkshire accent. So, when the producers cast him as Ned Stark, his cadence fit right in with damp, gray Winterfell and its environs. However, the northern accent was an affectation for Kit

Harington, as his London enunciation seemed incongruous with that of a bastard son (or so we were told) of a northern lord. So Jon Snow wasn't able to develop the posh elocution of nobility. He did likely develop a taste for northern brews, though. And he would have felt right at home when he moved to the Wall and took the Black. But he likely wouldn't get drunk too often—a good thing when all that stands between the realm and utter annihilation from the North is a ragtag group of bastards and criminals. More often than not, the brothers of the Night's Watch were sipping "small beer." No, they weren't drinking out of thimbles. Small beer is a lower-ABV brew that traditionally has been made from what brewers have called the "second runnings" of a much stronger beer, such as a barley wine. When the brewers have removed the wort from the barley wine's mash, they'd add warm water to the mash to make the lighter beer. It's like when you reuse a teabag. There's still some tea to be had, but it's likely to be considerably weaker.

Barley wine was quite common during the medieval period, so it fits quite comfortably into the *Song of Ice and Fire/Game of Thrones* world. Tyrion Lannister, on the lam after his wrongful conviction for the murder of his nephew, King Joffrey, in the fifth book, *A Dance with Dragons*, described the Night's Watch to a washerwoman thusly: "…no sweet, freaky wives to warm your bed at night, only cold winds, salted cod and small beer." Actually, sounds like the perfect Christmas Eve to me.

Small beer is also quite common north of the Wall, which is kind of a no-brainer, considering that most of the wildlings don't have two coins to rub together and they've really got to stretch their brews. That's especially true when you keep spawning kids and marrying dozens of your own offspring. When Jon and crew first meet with the incestuous, serial daughter impregnator Craster in book two, *A Clash of Kings*, the wildling patriarch is drinking what's described as "thin, yellow beer." It's young Snow's first meeting with a wildling—or "free folk" as they prefer to call themselves—and Jon's a bit underwhelmed after growing up with Winterfell servant (and Hodor's great-grandmother) Old Nan's tall tales of savages who drank blood from human skulls. (Personally, I'm good with just the beer.)

Small beer, over the centuries, has gotten a bit of a bad rap. In fact, it found a place in the British vernacular beyond its brewing origins. "Small beer" has come to mean insignificant or, if you prefer consumable analogies, "small potatoes."

But the style has made something of a comeback as lower-ABV session beers have become all the rage. A number of brewers market small beers between 2 and 2.5 percent ABV. Anchor Brewing in San Francisco even produces a brand named "Small Beer," though it's just above 3 percent ABV. The small beers of yore were more commonly between 1 and 2 percent ABV—sometimes as low as 0.5 percent.

Of course, as is the case in the continent of Europe in our reality, there's plenty of overlap, particularly in the south. Since grains can grow just about anywhere, southern Westeros isn't wine-exclusive. The underclasses, especially, consume beer because it's generally cheaper to produce, based on raw material availability. On the distilled spirits side, there's a common disparity of whiskey distilling versus brandy distilling. It takes between five hundred and eight hundred pounds of grain to make a barrel of whiskey. For the same volume of brandy, it takes between six thousand and ten thousand pounds of fruit.

THE SPIRIT OF THE TIMES

I'm a bit surprised that rum has popped up a few times on the pages of Martin's epic book series. When Samwell Tarly and Gilly were sailing on the vessel, the *Cinnamon Wind*, they drank from a cask of spiced rum—the first time Sam had consumed the spirit. It struck him as "strange and heady."

Tyrion also made a couple of references to rum, noting that one could get drunk more quickly on the molasses spirit than on wine, and that the aforementioned "piss" tastes better than "the black tar rum that sailors drink."

If the era of *A Song of Ice and Fire* is meant to be a stand-in for the Middle Ages, there really wasn't a whole lot of distilling going on. Sure, evidence suggests that distillation may have developed in the Middle East as early as three thousand years ago, but the practice of distilling alcoholic beverages didn't start in earnest until the late medieval period. And there really wasn't anything resembling rum until at least the late fifteenth century—certainly nothing that was common enough to show up by the barrel full on sailors' ships. It kind of supports my theory that Westeros is actually in the far future—why else would you have summers and winters that last close to a decade? Climate change, of course!

WINTER IS BREWING

A selection of Brewery Ommegang's *Game of Thrones* beers
Photo Credit: Mike Falco/Brewery Ommegang (special thanks to HBO)

An epic television drama demands an equally epic beer series, and, if there is ever a master class on how to do a licensed pop culture beverage tie-in, the team at Brewery Ommegang in Cooperstown, New York, should be the ones running it! Ommegang rose to the challenge when it hooked up with HBO in 2012 to craft a range of *Game of Thrones*-branded brews, all with elements inspired by the TV series. Ommegang, a unit of Belgium-based Duvel Moortgat, released the inaugural beer in the spring of 2013 in time for the debut episode of season three. Iron Throne blonde ale was the first one out of the gate (or, rather, out of brew master Phil Leinhart's brew house). Its hue was a reference to the golden locks of the Lannister family, who sat on the Iron Throne for most of the series' run. The idea was that it was soft and fair in appearance, but with a sneaky bite—pretty much Cersei in a nutshell. Ommegang continued to release *Game of Thrones* beers for the rest of the show's run on HBO, averaging two per year. Subsequent releases included:

- Take the Black Stout, a rich, 7.0 percent ABV dark brew inspired by the Night's Watch.

- Fire and Blood, a 6.8 percent ABV red ale that was a nod to Daenerys Targaryen.

- Valar Morghulis ("all men must die" in High Valerian), an 8 percent ABV Abbey Dubbel featuring the two-headed coin Jaqen H'ghar gave Arya.

- Three-Eyed Raven, a 7.2 percent dark saison and a bit of a shout-out to young Bran Stark.

- Seven Kingdoms, a 6.9 percent ABV, hazy yellow hoppy wheat ale.

- Valar Dohaeris ("all men must serve"), a Belgian-style tripel, a sequel of sorts to Valar Morghulis, was inspired by Arya's ordeal at the House of Black and White. The strength, 9 percent ABV, is masked by its lighter appearance. Just like Arya.

- Bend the Knee, a 9 percent ABV strong golden ale released with three separate label designs—each featuring a different House's sigil: Stark, Targaryen, or Lannister.

- My Watch Has Ended, an 8 percent ABV imperial brown ale brewed with maple syrup and fenugreek, released to commemorate the end of the HBO series and, consequently, the end of the beer series.

Ommegang also released the Royal Reserve Collection, a series of four brews released in 2018, the only year Game of Thrones was absent from TV screens during its entire eight-season run:

- Hand of the Queen, Tyrion Lannister's brew, is a big, boozy barley wine. What else would you want when you drink and you know things?

- Queen of the Seven Kingdoms, a sour blonde ale, which, you guessed it, is another one brewed for our favorite sour blonde, Cersei.

- Mother of Dragons is another one brewed especially for Dany Targaryen. It's a blend of smoked porter and Belgian kriek (the fiery part).

- King in the North, in honor of Jon Snow, is a barrel-aged imperial stout, which is what you'd really want on a chilling night on the Wall or around Winterfell.

IRON AND WINE

Since wine is just as an important part of the Ice and Fire universe, it was only a matter of time before a vintner produced a line of *Game of Thrones* reds and whites. Fourth-generation grape grower and winemaker Bob Cabral rose to the (fully licensed) challenge with a 2015 vintage Napa Valley Cabernet Sauvignon, a 2016 Central Coast Chardonnay, 2016 Oregon Pinot Noir, and a Paso Robles red blend. Most of them retail for an accessible $19.99—with the exception of the Napa Cab, which sells for $49.99. The labels are fairly elegant and not over the top, so "classy" wine folks won't be scared away.

YOU KNOW NOTHING, JOHNNIE SNOW

I stand by my earlier assertion that distilled spirits have little place in a medieval world, but I still think it's cool that Diageo has partnered with HBO on the release of a series of limited-edition *Game of Thrones* Scotch whisky expressions. The first was White Walker by Johnnie Walker blended whiskey, released in late 2018 ahead of the TV iteration's final season (and who knows how far ahead of the release of Martin's supposed final two books that might as well be named "Godot"). The brand encourages drinkers to freeze the bottle for a special message—the chill activates the label's thermos-chromatic ink.

As strange as a *Game of Thrones* whiskey may seem, the wintry White Walkers theme is somewhat on brand. One could argue that the world beyond the Wall—from where the Walkers have been descending—is the Westerosi equivalent of Scotland. And that makes a lot of sense, considering the often-contentious relationship between the English and Scottish throughout history. Hey, don't kill the messenger.

Diageo followed up the release of the White Walker blend with a range of single malts in early 2019. The lineup harnessed the whiskey stocks of some of the most iconic distilleries within Diageo's portfolio—and within all of Scotland, for that matter:

- House Stark—Dalwhinnie Winter's Frost

- House Tully—Singleton of Glendullan Select

- House Targaryen—Cardhu Gold Reserve

- House Lannister—Lagavulin, nine-year-old

- The Night's Watch—Oban Bay Reserve

- House Greyjoy—Talisker Select Reserve

- House Baratheon—Royal Lochnagar, twelve-year-old

- House Tyrell—Clynelish Reserve

BLOODY MELISANDRE

Of course, the boozy tribute to The Red Woman has to be a riff on a classic Bloody Mary. But there's no vodka to be found in this version. I've swapped out the neutral spirit in favor of the Dutch spirit jenever—it's a nod to the actress who plays Melisandre on the TV version of George R.R. Martin's epic book series, Netherlands native Carice van Houten. There's also a little bit of balsamic vinegar and black olive juice, as well as a black olive garnish, because the night is dark and full of terrors. I've also included a bit of smoke because: a) she likes to burn things, and b) when she's not burning things, she's summoning smoke demons to kill wannabe kings.

- Wood chip or toothpick for smoke
- 2 ounces oude genever
- ½ ounce juice from can of black olives
- ½ ounces balsamic vinegar
- ½ teaspoon hot sauce (double or triple that if you want it spicier)
- 8 ounces tomato juice (If you can get your hands on some San Marzano tomatoes, use the juice from the can. Keep in mind that you'll have to add more salt if you're not using branded tomato juice.)
- ¾ ounce fresh lime juice (from ¾ of a lime; save remaining ¼ for garnish)
- ½ teaspoon celery salt
- ¼ teaspoon black pepper, more to taste
- 4 black olives (garnish)

Place four to five cubes of ice at the bottom of a large glass, like a shaker pint. Light the toothpick or wood chip until it ignites. Let it burn for about three seconds and then snuff it out by dropping it on the ice cubes. Cover the mouth of the glass with a saucer or coaster. Let the smoke from the smoldering wood engulf the inside of the glass and the ice for at least a minute. Remove the coaster or saucer. Pour in jenever, olive juice, balsamic vinegar, hot sauce, and tomato juice (in that order). Stir well. Squeeze the ¾ lime into the drink and add pepper and celery salt. Stir again. Garnish with lime quarter and a toothpick with four black olives. Serve.

(A SONG OF) ICE AND FIRE

Here's another cocktail from our friend Ben Paré at the Fontainebleau in Miami, Florida. It's a variation on the classic Blood and Sand, featuring one of the *Game of Thrones* limited-edition Scotch whiskies.

- 1 ounce Johnnie Walker "White Walker" Scotch whisky
- 1 ounce fresh-squeezed orange juice
- 1 ounce sweet vermouth (Ben recommends Antica Formula)
- 1 ounce Cherry Heering

Combine all ingredients in a mixing glass, stir, and serve up with a flamed orange peel.

BASTARD'S SOUR

Here's a tropical concoction created by "Tiki Commando" Jason Alexander (not George Costanza), proprietor of Tacoma, Washington's Devil's Reef. Alexander created it in partnership with Beeline Creative, a.k.a. Geeki Tikis, to fill Geeki's Jon Snow mug.

- 2 ounces Plantation Xaymaca Rum
- ½ ounce Pierre Ferrand Dry Curaçao
- 1½ ounces orange juice
- 1 ounce lemon juice
- ½ ounce orgeat
- ½ ounce honey syrup

Add all ingredients to a mixing tin and flash blend or shake with a can of crushed ice for five seconds. Pour unstrained into the mug. Garnish with a mint sprig and orchid. Dust with powdered sugar to simulate snow, as in "You know nothing, Jon…"

Bastard's Sour (in Geeki Tikis Jon Snow mug). Photo Credit: Devil's Reef Tacoma (special thanks to Beeline Creative)

CHAPTER 6
EXPECTO INTOXICATUM!

We have to have a serious conversation about underage drinking. Okay, maybe not so serious. Go binge watch family-friendly '80s and early '90s sitcoms like *Growing Pains* or *Saved by the Bell* when "very special episodes" served up such themes with a side of laugh track.

Still, when I first read *Harry Potter and the Prisoner of Azkaban*—and I'm sure I'm not the only one who thought this—my eyebrows raised a bit when the magic kids started rhapsodizing about butterbeer. I know, I know, the version that they serve at the Wizarding World of Harry Potter in Orlando is completely sans alcohol, but the theme park managers know which side their bread is buttered on (pun intended). The park sold a million mugs of the stuff by 2011, a year after it opened. As of fall 2018, volume surpassed twenty million units. The Wizarding World would never have been able to hit those kinds of numbers with a beverage that was targeted only to parents and the childless, Potter-obsessed adults who make regular pilgrimages to the Sunshine State attraction. So, the real-world version is just a butterscotch-y riff on the cream soda, sarsaparilla, and root beer genre of soft drinks. But it's not quite so cut-and-dried on the pages of the young adult fantasy book series, or in the film adaptations for that matter. J.K. Rowling has been generally coy about it. But there are clues, here and there, that her beloved butterbeer actually has a bit of booze in it.

The mythical butterbeer. Photo Credit: iStock by Getty Images

First of all, house-elves have been known to get tanked on the stuff. One could credibly argue that the beverage has an oddly intoxicating effect that's unique to house-elf physiology, much in the same way that sour milk got the melon-headed extraterrestrials hammered in the 1988 film, *Alien Nation*. I'm not a fan of that theory, mainly because Potter is a British franchise, and Brits tend to be a bit less pearl-clutchy about drinks with trace amounts of alcohol in them. (And house-elves are like a foot tall, so they're likely to get drunk faster than average-size humans.) In the UK, it's not considered a breakdown of traditional societal values when parents bring their kids to a pub. It's part of the culture.

Ginger beer is also part of the Brits' culture. What most Americans don't realize is that ginger beers brewed in the eighteenth and nineteenth centuries actually had some alcohol in them. Their ABVs were considerably lower than that of English ales—1 to 2 percent, versus traditional British beer proper's 4 percent—but I wouldn't call it negligible. If you look at an authentic German Berliner Weiss, those seldom went much above 2.9 percent.

True ginger beer is brewed and fermented much like ales and lagers are, with the yeast converting some of the sugar into alcohol naturally. Most ginger beers produced in that manner today have their alcohol removed in the same way that booze is removed from alcohol-free beer. A fraction of traditional makers leave the ethanol intact. Other producers make ginger beer through a manufacturing process that doesn't involve brewing or fermentation.

I don't know Madam Rosmerta too well, but the proprietor of the Three Broomsticks in Hogsmeade has been known to make a pretty mean oak-aged mead—the fermented honey drink that is very likely the world's oldest alcoholic drink. She hardly strikes me as someone who would go through the trouble of removing trace amounts of alcohol from her butterbeer just to appease occasional excursions into town by the Hogwarts crew. She'd make a hell of a lot more money off of the professors and staff—Hagrid's certainly no teetotaler—than she would off of the underage students who likely have very little money of their own (save for Harry, who inherited his knuts, sickles, and galleons from his Voldemort-murdered parents). And, in the wizarding world, adulthood officially begins at seventeen. I'd imagine that would be the legal drinking age as well—not that Rosmerta's checking IDs anyway, since Harry, Hermione, and Ron were sipping their suds at the age of thirteen.

Our heroes, on occasion, have hinted at the presence of alcohol in butterbeer. In *Harry Potter and the Goblet of Fire*, Dobby more or less throws his fellow house-elf, Winky, under the Knight Bus, when Dobby tells Harry that Winky's "getting through six bottles a day now." Harry points out that it's "not strong," to which Dobby replies, "'tis strong for a house-elf." Notice that Harry doesn't say "there isn't any booze in it," but that it's "not strong." You could say the same for a pilsner (5-ish percent) in relation to, say, a barley wine (10 percent to infinity). But you'd still understand that enough pilsners could get you drunk. It's plausible that six butterbeers is an alarming quantity for a species that weighs about fifteen pounds—roughly the equivalent of a twenty-four-bottle case of lager to a human drinker of average weight.

We can debate the alcohol content—or lack thereof—until we're blue in the face and still not come to any sort of consensus. But one beverage whose potency is beyond question is firewhisky. You won't find any witches and wizards under the age of seventeen buying this stuff legally. As its name suggests, it's a grain-based distillate with a healthy helping of spice in it. The closest thing we have to it in the muggle world is probably Fireball, the cinnamon-flavored whiskey that's generally for people who don't like to drink whiskey at all. However, the Potterized version seems to be considerably rougher around the edges. There are also a few white whale brands to chase that are known to be stronger than others. Ogden's Old is, perhaps, the best known and a personal favorite of the insufferable grandstander and tall-tale-teller, Gilderoy Lockhart. (I always wish his fate in the movies was as tragic as it was in the books.)

The Hog's Head Inn, the Hopping Pot, and the Leaky Cauldron in the Wizarding World theme park's version of Hogsmeade carry muggle-friendly Blishen's Cinnamon Flavoured Firewhisky. Non-wizarding types purportedly can't handle the flagship Blishen's Firewhisky, a thirty-nine-year-old Highland Scotch whisky.

The movie version of the Leaky Cauldron—but not the literary iteration—served something known as Beetle Berry Whiskey. Shame on the producers for allowing that to happen!

Not much is known about where and how this stuff is made, but the assumption is that its distillate base is made with the eponymous berries. That would make it a brandy, not a whiskey, since berries are fruits and not grains. It really makes me wonder what J.K. Rowling has to say about this. She's got some Scottish blood in her and she spends much of her time in Scotland (where she completed the book series). I want to give the filmmakers the benefit of the doubt, that they meant it as a whiskey flavored with beetled berries, but I'm not hopeful. Besides, that would make it a whiskey liqueur and not a whiskey proper.

In the film version—again, not the book—of *Harry Potter and the Half-Blood Prince*, the Three Broomsticks stocks a spirit known as Dragon Barrel Brandy. So, fruit-based distillates (i.e. brandies) are definitely a thing in the wizarding world. Not much is known about its contents, but it's made in Paris, so it's likely somewhere in the Cognac and Armagnac families. There's no shortage of grapes in Paris, so I can't imagine how Dragon Barrel would even compete if it were any other fruit. One thing that we do know is that, according to its label, it spent 1,800 months (150 years) in barrels. That's not as outlandish as it sounds because many of the major Cognac houses have rare bottlings of brandies that are well over a century, even more than two centuries old. Guinness World Records recognized Cognac Gautier 1762 as the oldest Cognac sold at public auction. It was bottled at 250 years old and sold in New York in 2014 for $59,500. (It's kind of a bargain when you consider just how old it is. Marie Antoinette was seven years old when the stuff went into oak.)

The only real difference between a super-old brandy in the real world and one in the wizarding world, is that the person who distilled the latter is very likely still alive. You know, magic.

Butterbeer and the wizard-made spirits are the two extremes of the Potterific booze spectrum. There's a whole vast continuum of tipples of all strengths in between those end points. When Bellatrix Lestrange and Narcissa Malfoy dropped in on Professor Snape at the beginning of both the book and film versions of *Harry Potter and the Half-Blood Prince*, we learned that old double-agent Severus liked to stock red elf-made wine. I'd imagine that house-elves had become quite adept at winemaking, since they were forced to perform all manner of household tasks for the wizardly upper crust, and I can't imagine the likes of Lucius Malfoy would want to get his hands dirty making his own wine. He'd probably also stain his platinum blonde locks.

BUTTERBEER'S OLDER BROTHER

We may never know the true alcohol content (or lack thereof) of butterbeer, but no one's ever going to confuse this cocktail with a kid's drink. This one comes from my neck of the woods: Alexandria, Virginia. Joseph Quintero is the beverage director of a local café and bar (with a kickass view of the Potomac) called Café 44. Joseph created this one as a boozy nod to the wizarding world. It's got the requisite butterscotch, but it's also got considerably more bourbon.

- 1½ ounces Wild Turkey 101 bourbon
- ¾ ounce lemon juice
- ½ ounce butterscotch syrup
- 4 drops of mole bitters
- Ginger beer (to top off)
- Cinnamon (garnish)
- Apple cider foam

Build in a cocktail shaker. Shake bourbon, lemon juice, butterscotch syrup, and bitters together, and strain over fresh ice. Top with ginger beer, but leave about a ¼ inch for the apple cider foam. Add the foam and garnish with a dusting of cinnamon.

Photo Credit: Nicki Lewis

FIFTH YEAR BUTTERBEER

Here's an alternative take on a butterbeer cocktail, courtesy of Fontainebleau's Ben Paré.

- 1½ ounce butterscotch schnapps (or homemade butterscotch syrup)
- 1 ounce browned butter-washed spiced rum (details below)
- 12 ounces cream ale (Boddingtons is a good option)

Combine all ingredients in a pint glass. Swizzle and serve.

For the browned butter-washed spiced rum—in a medium-sized skillet, melt 1 stick of butter over medium heat. Once melted, stir the butter semi-frequently until the milk solids begin to turn brown (you will smell a sweet, nutty aroma), about two to three minutes. In a heat-safe container, immediately combine browned butter with one bottle of spiced rum of choice. Infuse at room temperature for three days, shaking every so often. Freeze overnight to resolidify butter. Scoop the hardened browned butter off the top of the container and pour the rum back into the bottle.

Pro Tip: You can now use the rum-infused browned butter you scooped from the top in a recipe of your choice! Ben's favorite is banana bread.

FIREWHISKEY OLD FASHIONED

This recipe is one of mine. No, I'm not going to suggest that you sully an old fashioned with Fireball or any such flavored whiskey. We're going to be making our own fire here—two kinds, in fact. First, there's the figurative fire in the form of hot pepper simple syrup. Then there's the actual kind, from the flamed orange peel. You'll need a match or lighter.

- 2 ounces rye or bourbon whiskey
- 1 teaspoon chili pepper simple syrup (Recipe below)
- 3 dashes hot pepper bitters (Dugan & Dane Bitter Ghost Pepper Bitters, Hella Smoked Chili Bitters, and Bittermens Hellfire Habanero Shrub are among those that would do the trick)
- 1 teaspoon of water
- Thin slice of orange peel

Put the simple syrup, bitters, and teaspoon of water at the bottom of an old fashioned glass and mix until everything is seamlessly merged. Add the whiskey and stir again. Place a large cube or sphere of ice in the mixture. Now, take the sliver of orange peel between the finger and thumb of your non-dominant hand and bend so the peel side is facing outward. Hold over the glass and then briefly ignite the outer peel, allowing some of the heated peel oil to drip into the glass. When the flame is out, rub the orange peel around the rim of the glass and drop in.

Photo Credit: Jeff Cioletti

For the chili pepper simple syrup—boil 1 cup of water in a pan and then stir 1 cup of sugar into the boiling water. Don't stop stirring for a good three minutes. Add 3 sliced jalapeño or habanero peppers into the liquid and reduce heat. Let simmer for about twenty minutes. Remove from heat and strain out the pepper pieces.

CHAPTER 7
DEAD DRUNK

Zombie entertainment has become a genre unto itself. We have the late George A. Romero to thank for giving birth to it, and we can thank the creative team behind *The Walking Dead* and its many iterations on page and on screen for keeping it alive—or, should I say, undead? I know Mr. Romero is probably turning over in his grave here, but I'm going to be focusing on *The Walking Dead* for this chapter. (Romero, not long before he shuffled off this mortal coil, reportedly had some choice words for *The Walking Dead.*) I'm going to talk primarily about the TV version of the zombie franchise because the continuity gets a little wonky when you try to move back and forth between the graphic novel series and the AMC show. And, well, it is one of the most watched—at times *the* most watched—scripted series on television.

The flagship *Walking Dead* TV series has, since its 2010 debut episode, been filmed in and around Atlanta, Georgia, and set in the Peach State for the first four and a half years of its run. One of the most visible craft brewers in Atlanta, SweetWater Brewing, made sure that its brand would live on well into the post-apocalyptic world. Eagle-eyed drinkers who watched the show during those early seasons will have spotted the SweetWater logo on untouched cases still sitting on long-abandoned supermarket shelves. The brewery had an ongoing relationship with the series' set designers which ensured product placement in an America where no new products were actually being made.

Photo Credit: Jeff Cioletti

The move turned out to be a social media bonanza for SweetWater, which boasted thousands of impressions thanks to the blink-and-you'll-miss-it moments.

But product placement is only a tiny part of the *Walking Dead* drinking story. If there's one thing I've learned from the franchise it's that humanity's complicated relationship with alcohol continues long after there's not much of humanity left. In the *Walking Dead* universe, drinking is, at alternating moments, both celebrated and vilified. You know, how it is every day in (at press time) the zombie-less world in which we currently live.

Some characters wrestle with their demons in a bottle. Hershel Greene is the most notable of those individuals. When we first encounter the farmstead patriarch, he's rather standoffish toward outsiders, particularly Rick Grimes and his merry band of survivors (very few of whom continued to survive much longer). He also has this misguided notion that walkers are still people and need to be saved. Hershel, his family, and friends would round up the zombies in the woods, harness them, and corral them in a rickety old barn. Team Grimes's "Shoot 'em in the head first, ask questions later" approach to walker management is the work of godless barbarians, as far as the Greenes are concerned. The holier-than-thou Hershel of season two is a far cry from the more evolved Hershel of seasons three and four.

We learn that much of his self-righteousness stems from his struggle to overcome alcoholism. In fact, he was, once upon a time, a hot mess before he got sober. That finally occurred, Hershel's daughter Maggie tells us, the day she was born. And, after many years of sobriety, he briefly falls off the wagon when he's forced to confront the reality that there really is no hope left. Rick and Glenn ultimately bring him back from the edge.

A couple of seasons later we meet Bob Stookey, whom we learn also is a problem drinker. But where Hershel has managed to keep his at bay for decades (with one minor blip), Bob carries his addiction from the world that was into the world that is— some rather difficult excess baggage to have to deal with when you have to spend the majority of your days beating back decaying monsters that are trying to eviscerate and eat you. It also doesn't help that a bottle of Jack Daniel's isn't actually considered "essential rations" when you're never sure whether you're ever going to eat again.

We learn in Bob's first episode (the season four premiere, "30 Days Without an Accident") that he's an alcoholic. When he's on a supply run at a deserted big box store with Daryl Dixon and crew, Bob surreptitiously makes a beeline to the booze aisle. He hesitates, but ultimately grabs a bottle to hide in his jacket. After a while, he comes to his senses and tries to place the bottle back on the shelf. In doing so, he inadvertently makes the entire rack come crashing down, trapping himself beneath it. The others eventually rescue him, but not without paying a huge price. Zach, Beth Greene's boyfriend of the moment, becomes walker food during the effort to save Bob. We're back to zero days without an accident.

It's a rather important scene, more important than most people give it credit for. It was an action-packed nail-biter, of course, and eminently entertaining, but it packed quite a moral punch. It reflected the destruction that alcoholism leaves in one's wake—and the sometimes irreparable damage it does to those individuals in an alcoholic's orbit. (Although I make a living writing about booze, I believe in moderation and that alcoholism is a serious affliction that needs to be treated as such). Bob drank to ease the pain caused by the trauma he experienced of living in zombie apocalyptic times. Ultimately, though, it's not Bob's addiction that does him in, but a walker bite (which he reveals to a group of Terminus cannibals chowing down on the "tainted meat" that is his leg).

To balance some of those heavier plotlines, *The Walking Dead* TV series offers a few social drinking moments of varying significance. One of the most bittersweet moments is when Beth has her first drink. It's an earnest grasp at a sense of normalcy— in this case, a typical young adult's inaugural experience with booze—in a world for which "normal" is a long-faded memory.

At the conclusion of the episode, immediately prior to season four's two-month halftime, the resurgent governor and his newly minted minions attempt to drive the protagonists from their prison home. The baddies don't succeed, but the damage they cause is irreversible. The prison is overrun with walkers and no longer inhabitable. And Hershel's dead—his neck met the business end of the governor's machete. The chaos that ensues causes our heroes to scatter in multiple directions, mostly in groups of two or three.

One of the show's unlikely pairs is Daryl and Beth, who are the sole stars of season four's twelfth episode, "Still." When we catch up with the awkward duo, they're running from place to place, hiding from walkers in the trunks of rotting cars, and subsisting on snakes and anything else that Daryl's able to skin alive. The constant struggle to find acceptable food and shelter has distracted Beth from grieving over her recently decapitated father. No words of dialogue are exchanged between the two in the opening minutes of "Still," save for a muttered "come on" from Daryl. After a lengthy montage of water-bottle scavenging, reptile slaughtering, and campfire starting, Beth, sitting a good seven feet from her traveling companion at their makeshift campsite, finally breaks the uncomfortable silence with "I need a drink." Daryl throws her a canteen. "No, I mean a real drink. As in alcohol."

Those youthful urges to experiment and rebel don't seem to recede. And Beth, being the daughter of a recovering alcoholic, has never been able to quench those thirsts. But, she points out, Hershel's "not exactly around anymore, so…" But it's more than curiosity. Beth is desperate to connect with the grunting, laconic Georgia tracker, if for no other reason than to break up the silent monotony of the desperate situation in which they find themselves. It gives them a mission, an adventure—call it a project—to find a little bit of booze to feed what is, for Beth, a rite of passage of sorts (not to mention a quest to keep her grief at bay). Initially, Daryl expresses zero interest in such a plan but eventually he comes around.

Their first stop is the nineteenth hole at the Pine Vista Country Club. ("Golfers like to booze it up, right?" Beth asks.) She finds a bottle of peach schnapps and asks if the artificially flavored liqueur is good. Without missing a beat, Daryl tells her "no." Beth points out that it's the only thing left, so it'll work just fine for her. She has no frame of reference anyway.

I can almost relate. Peach schnapps wasn't the first drink I ever had, but a mini bottle of it was a "gift" on my twenty-first birthday when I was buying alcohol for the very first time (the emphasis on "buying"). When the clerk at my college town liquor store looked at my driver's license (which I proudly, triumphantly handed to him), he said, "Happy Birthday!" and threw in the 50-ml of the most prominent ingredient in the Fuzzy Navel. So, in a sense, the sickeningly sweet, syrupy liqueur was my own boozy rite of passage.

I was stocking up for my colleagues at my college newspaper. My fellow editors at *The Daily Targum* and I often would celebrate the completion of the day's issue with a couple of drinks in the office. So it's very likely that I didn't even drink the peach schnapps—someone else probably grabbed it out of the bag when I returned to the newsroom—which gives me something else in common with Beth, because neither did she. She couldn't find a clean glass in the post-apocalyptic pub and resigned herself to drinking straight from the bottle. But before she could get it open, she broke down. The tears she hadn't had a moment to cry since her father's untimely passing finally caught up with her. Beth's emotional moment is what finally moves Daryl—enough to smash the bottle out of her hand before she's able to take a single sip. "You ain't gonna have your first drink be no damn peach schnapps," he explains. He's going to show her how to drink the Dixon way and leads her to an abandoned shack in the woods that Daryl once found with Michonne. Beth thought he was taking her to a liquor store. "This is better," Daryl tells her. Inside, he presents her with his secret stash: a crate full of mason jars and glass jugs of moonshine. He pours Beth her *real* first drink. She's a bit apprehensive at first because Hershel once told her that bad moonshine could make you go blind.

He wasn't wrong. That may seem like an urban legend that parents spread to scare their kids into not drinking. But blindness was a big problem during Prohibition with all of the sketchy bathtub gin being made. Methanol was the usual culprit where that was concerned. Ethanol is the stuff that's safe to drink. Methanol, not so much. During the distilling process, the first bits of alcohol to come through the still contain methanol, and distillers typically remove it. But if the moonshiner is a lousy distiller, they'll leave a little too much methanol in the finished product. The really unsavory sort would add methanol to the mix to make the stuff stronger. But Daryl knows this is the good stuff and, besides, he says, "nothin' worth seein' out there anymore anyway."

After her initial sip, Beth reveals that it's the most disgusting thing she's ever tasted—before downing the remaining contents of her glass and pouring a second round. Daryl refuses to join her at first because he needs to be sharp to keep watch. But this displeases Beth because it makes Daryl seem like her chaperone. There's a walker outside, so they decide to stick around in the distiller's shack and Daryl finally agrees to make the best of the situation. That situation evolves into a drinking game—a foreign concept to Daryl because he's "never needed a game to get lit before"—and then eventually into a shouting match, because isn't that how all drinking games end?

More critically, what we witness is an entire platonic relationship evolving with an intense bond forming between these two folks from vastly different sides of the tracks. And it's all over drinks. Most of us remember our first drinking experience to some extent. Mine was during my first week of college, in the dorm room of a woman I was trying to impress (unsuccessfully) who lived down the hall from me. It was the first time I had ever heard of Everclear, and in this case it was mixed with red Kool-Aid. I suspect that Beth's moment would've been even more memorable had her life not had a premature expiration date. It was just as much of a touchstone for Daryl, as it's what drove him to find Beth at any cost after she was abducted shortly after they tossed back a few. It's that much more devastating when she essentially dies in his arms.

DIPLOMACY

Much as in *Star Trek*'s very optimistic future, fancy, hard-to-get booze also is a diplomatic tool in the very hopeless world of *The Walking Dead*. The moment that communities begin to rise from the ashes of the decimated Earth, adversaries parlay over some damned good Scotch. In the season three episode "Arrow on the Doorpost," Andrea (ill-advisedly) brokers a meeting between Rick and the governor (the local despot she's been boning) to get them to settle their differences once and for all and to figure out a way that the two communities—Rick and co.'s prison and the governor's Woodbury—can coexist in peace. To call the summit "tense" would be understating things greatly. The governor tries to cut the tension inside the Verlin Feed & Seed by declaring, "I brought whiskey!" The villain pours glasses for both of them at first, but only the governor drinks initially. Who could blame him? Who wants to be poisoned?

Rick does eventually drink—the whiskey was untainted—acknowledging that his nemesis is starting to get inside his head. The governor has just finished telling Rick how the former lost his wife, some time before the apocalypse. He was at work, "taking shit from a boss half my age and an IQ even lower" when someone called to inform him that his wife had been in a fatal accident. The governor knowingly touched a nerve in Rick, as Rick had just lost his own wife mere weeks prior during childbirth. The one-eyed antagonist lamented how he let an earlier, innocuous call from his wife go to voicemail, not realizing it'd be the last chance he'd ever get to speak to her. It's an obvious manipulation, meant to throw Rick off balance. And it works just enough to get him to pick up a glass and sip some whiskey. The bottle's label is intentionally obscured, likely due to no product placement deal with the distillery. Given the shape of the bottle, bourbon is the likely choice, and my educated guess about its specific contents would be Old Pogue.

Scotch whisky, as opposed to bourbon, is the tipple of choice of another would-be diplomat, Gregory, figurehead of the Hilltop community in seasons seven and eight. Calling Gregory's brand of inter-colony relations "diplomacy" is way too generous. He's basically post-apocalyptic Virginia's answer to Neville Chamberlain. Not the actual Neville Chamberlain, but George Costanza's version, the famously spineless British prime minister who would give up half of Europe if you dunked him in a toilet. Gregory was desperate to kiss the asses of his oppressors, the Saviors, a.k.a. Negan and his cronies, and would throw under the bus any member of his community who got in his sniveling way. When Negan's chief enforcer, Simon, paid Gregory a visit (never a social call), Gregory's head was so far up Simon's ass, he could give the menacing henchman a full dental exam. It's the same dynamic that probably plays out during Donald Trump's private meetings with Vladimir Putin.

At the time of Simon's visit, Maggie and Sasha are hiding out at the Hilltop—and Gregory doesn't exactly welcome them with open arms. In fact, he is downright hostile to them even being there because it leaves the cowardly Hilltop leader vulnerable. When Simon asks him if there's anything Gregory wants to tell him—"any hitches in the giddyap I should be aware of," in Simon's words—Gregory hesitates for a moment before he escorts Simon to a closet. Maggie and Sasha, Gregory believes, are inside that closet. If the spineless demagogue hands over the two fugitives, he might curry a little favor with the Negan empire. But as it turns out, it's not Maggie and Sasha in that cupboard, but a case of The Balvenie. Simon admits that he doesn't care much for Scotch ("tastes like ashtrays and window cleaner"), as he's a gin man. I can respect that. His boss, however, is going to love it—so much so that Simon wants to take all of the credit for the gesture (sorry, Gregory). Gregory tries to hold on to a bottle of his beloved whiskey, but Simon doesn't allow it. It's a nice little gut-punch for Gregory, who fancies himself a bit of a plutocrat (though he likely would never cop to such a distasteful term). He likes to wear fancy (for a zombie-ravaged society) sport jackets and leave all of the real work to the underlings while he sips his expensive Scotch (which is even more rare now that nothing's being imported from across the Atlantic). As much as we hate Simon, the Scotch incident was probably the one moment when we all cheered him on.

On a number of occasions, we're reminded of just how shitty a leader Gregory is when he can't seem to remember the names of people in the community. He apparently suffers no such selective amnesia when it comes to the favorite tipples of fascist minions. Later in season seven, in the episode "The Other Side," Simon and his crew pay another special visit to the Hilltop, not long after their regular pick-up trip. Gregory offers Simon some recently procured gin ("You're a gin man, right?"), but Simon reveals that he's into tequila now. "Añejo, reposado, sipping, mixing." A bit later in the episode, Simon invites Gregory to the Sanctuary if he ever feels like ratting on anyone who's giving him trouble. Simon would gladly listen to Gregory share a little intel over a couple of glasses of distilled agave goodness. Who said the Saviors were uncivilized?

FEAR THE WALKING DEAD

This is the part where I get to talk about the *Walking Dead* universe and not have to worry about pissing off a large contingent of "the comic books are better" people because there is no *Fear the Walking Dead* comic. It has existed solely on screen. While I'm a big fan of Victor Strand's boozy benders—particularly when he and Madison Clark bond over a few drinks at the bar in the Mexican hotel they're holed up in for a chunk of season two—there's a story line a couple of seasons later that likely tickled the sensibilities of more than a few beer geeks.

The back half of season four of *Fear the Walking Dead* is about the booziest the zombie genre has ever been, with an entire multi-episode arc devoted to a beer recipe. That's when we meet Jim. Every third word out of his mouth has something to do with fermented malt. We learn that, before the world got zombified (shout out to Alien Sex Fiend's song, "Now I'm Feeling Zombified"), Jim was a professional brewer—supposedly a damned good one. His brand, Augie's Ale, was one that folks in the Dead-iverse were supposed to have heard of.

In fact, he tells us, he had made a deal to sell his brewery to a "large multinational" (my money's on Anheuser-Busch InBev), just before the entire world went to hell. (Side note: it's moments like these that make me wonder if the billionaires who run AB InBev figured out a way to survive in the new normal, or whether they were an early feast for the walkers. I'd like to believe the latter).

"It took a lot to get there," Jim said. "Win all the right awards, get in all the right trade mags." (I was editor-in-chief of one of the biggest trade publications in the business at year zero of the outbreak, 2010. So, you're welcome, Jim.) "But it worked and I was about to cash in. I was going to be rich. But shit went to hell." Best laid plans, Jimbo. Best laid plans.

We also learn that if you're faced with a zombie apocalypse, the safest place to hole up for several years is inside a brewery. That worked for Jim for a time, but it also made him ill-equipped to deal with the world once he was forced to leave. His whiny, woe-is-me victim complex doesn't exactly endear him with his new traveling companions.

Jim's brewing expertise did give him a purpose in the post-apocalyptic world. And it was a purpose rooted in history. He even explains as much, noting that the course of human development has returned to a point in time when beer offers a safe and sterile source of hydration and nutrition. He notes that thousands of years before, humans were nomads but beer made us settle and learn agriculture. "Egyptians, Sumerians, Babylonians, Incans, the Chinese: beer, beer, beer, beer, beer."

He's absolutely right. Up until not too long ago, a person was more likely to die from drinking from the local water supply than they were to be sufficiently hydrated. Beer was a safer way to achieve hydration. For one thing, there's a lengthy boiling process involved, so most unwelcome microbes are exterminated. Alpha acids in hops also possess certain antimicrobial properties. And then, of course, there's the alcohol, which takes care of more than a few harmful bacteria

Beer was also a source of nourishment. During long fasting periods in the Middle Ages and later, monks would consume only the beer they made. Beer is very rich in vitamins, believe it or not.

And, it provided nourishment of a different kind: human connection and comfort.

Jim leaves a bottle of Augie's Ale in one of the "Take What You Need, Leave What You Don't" boxes on the side of the road. Luciana (who is initially introduced as a love interest for Nick Clark, but ultimately proves, by outliving him, that she's better at the whole survival thing) encounters a badly injured man pinned inside his car after a crash. The man, Clayton, has been there for quite a while and can't be moved because the wrecked vehicle is pretty much all that's holding his body together. He tells Luciana that all he wants is a beer. She makes it her mission to find him one.

After mostly coming up empty, she finally happens upon the box and delivers it, triumphantly, to the dying Clayton. He marvels at the fact that it's actually cold, thanks to an ice pack inside a first-aid kit that shared the box with the beer. It was one last moment of enjoyment for Clayton before he expired. It made him experience, if only for a few minutes, a sense of normalcy in an abnormal world.

The beer offered comfort for Luciana, as well—not because she had just done a good deed, but because that simple, twelve-ounce bottle of Augie's Ale represented hope at a time and place where the concept seemed all but extinct.

Therefore, Jim, by nature of his chosen trade, stumbles into a way to make himself necessary in the walker-ravaged wasteland that planet Earth has become. As long as people know that, they'll be less likely to kill him for being annoying.

Despite his irritating victim complex, Jim ultimately redeems himself at the very end of his (natural) life when he, freshly bitten and doomed to die, jumps from a multi-story rooftop so he can land on a van below, trigger its alarm to distract a walker swarm, and allow his friends to escape. But before he does, he finally divulges his recipe to ex-Marine Sarah, who's been trying to get it from him since the moment they met (which wasn't exactly under friendly circumstances, to be honest).

The writers of *Fear the Walking Dead* have great attention to detail here. Normally, a booze fan could roll their eyes at the inaccuracies and misconceptions that many a pop culture property perpetuates when depicting favorite beverages. But Jim's laundry list of ingredients and his basic explanation of the brewing process kind of made me smile. He begins with "68 percent pils malt, 15 percent wheat malt" and even namechecks one of the world's best malt houses, Bamberg, Germany-based Weyermann. "7 percent flaked oats," he continues, "10 percent Vienna [malt]." Yes, the grain bill adds up to 100 percent. Then he moves on to the hops: "40 grams Slovenian pellets, 70 grams Czech Saaz whole hops"—the latter of which is my favorite varietal. "You need Belgian and French saison yeast," he adds. "You're gonna want to cook the mash at 151, 152 Fahrenheit. Then comes fermentation." Jim tells Sarah to pitch the yeast at 68 degrees Fahrenheit and ferment for ten days. He then tells Sarah to hold the walkie talkie to his ear so no one else will hear when he relays the "most important part." That remains a mystery.

Unfortunately, Sarah isn't the only one listening. Dirty-faced, deranged walker wrangler Martha, the closest thing to a lone wolf serial killer the *Walking Dead* universe has ever had, was eavesdropping. She found Jim's body and, just as he was about to turn, she wrote all of the ingredients on his face with a Sharpie. Now that's just plain disrespectful.

Luckily, as it turns out, Jim gets to have the last word. When our heroes simultaneously come down with a mystery stomach bug, we soon learn that Martha spiked cases-upon-cases of their bottled water with antifreeze. And, wouldn't you know, there's an everyday antidote to antifreeze poisoning: ethanol. No, I didn't know that either, but June (Jenna Elfman) was an experienced nurse and privy to that little tidbit. She explains that ethanol would stop their bodies from trying to metabolize the antifreeze.

It just so happens there's an abandoned tanker truck full of the stuff outside. (They're holed up in a gas station convenience store, so I'll allow it.) However, in their effort to fend off the walker horde that's surrounded the mini-mart, they shoot a few holes in the tanker, spilling all of its contents onto the ground. Now, at this point, I'm yelling at the screen. "Ethanol is in every adult beverage under the sun! Can't they find a bottle of booze somewhere?!" Oh, right, the writers underestimated the intelligence of their audience, assuming nobody knows ethanol's most pervasive commercial application. That is, until, a "booze ex machina" moment occurs. Stick-ninja Morgan arrives, just in the nick of time, and declares to his nearly dead compatriots, "Ethanol is just a fancy word for alcohol, right? I made a stop along the way." Parked outside is a side-load beverage delivery truck with Augie's Ale branding (Jim really was close to hitting the big time). And, wouldn't you know it, it was full. Beer saves the day.

"That's twice Jimbo saved our keisters," Sarah realizes.

She then toasts the sky, telling Jim, wherever he is, "here's to you, asshole." The stuff of life indeed.

ZOMBIES BREAK THE FOURTH WALL

The Walking Dead has sought to quench the thirst of some of its real-world devotees. The Atlanta brewery Sweetwater may have had some nifty product placement in the flagship series, but another Georgia producer, Terrapin Beer Co. in Athens, had the honor of bringing the series into the real world with its line of Walking Dead beers. The first of those was Blood Orange IPA (emphasis on the "Blood," of course). Dubbed by its makers "the official beer of the undead," Terrapin uses what it calls "a horrific amount of hops" combined with blood orange peel to craft this homage to the long-running, locally filmed AMC series. To really sell its zombie street cred, Terrapin recommended lots of innards and viscera as the perfect pairing companions: sweetbreads, chitterlings, and other offal offerings.

Terrapin took things up a notch when it followed up the release of Blood Orange IPA with the skull-splitting "Lucille"—an homage to Negan's trusty, barbed-wire-enhanced slugger. The Blackstrap Molasses Stout is aged with hickory, maple, and ash—the three woods used to make baseball bats. The label image features a wooden background covered in barbed wire, just in case you didn't get the reference. It's got an ABV upwards of 9 percent, so be careful not to lose your mind over this one. Terrapin—of which MillerCoors is now a majority owner— produced both Walking Dead beers in collaboration with the series' parent, Skybound Entertainment.

Some brewers never let the lack of a licensing deal get in the way of a good homage. Back in 2014, Dock Street Brewery in Philadelphia was so excited for TWD's fourth season finale that it brewed Walker beer (sans any visible overt branding tying it to the series, save for a generic zombie image on the label). Dock Street brewed Walker with malted wheat, oats, and flaked barley, as well as some organic cranberries. Oh, and smoked goat brains. I'm seriously not making that up!

CHAPTER 8
PIXELS & POTABLES

For most of the '80s, I seriously could have had my mail forwarded to the Fun Palace, the video arcade at Wayne Hills Mall in New Jersey. When I wasn't record and cassette shopping at Sam Goody, manhandling all of the *Doctor Who* Target novelizations at Waldenbooks, or dining at McDonald's (don't judge me), I was popping countless quarters (which I likely "borrowed" from my dad's not-so-secret money sock) into *Q-Bert, Donkey Kong, Tron, Dragon's Lair* (a scam of a game if there ever was one), Arkanoid, and many others. Oh, and how could I forget to mention *Tapper*, this being a booze book and all.

Most people of my generation probably remember it as *Root Beer Tapper*, the more family-friendly version. Originally, Anheuser-Busch sponsored the game as yet another facet of its ubiquitous point-of-sale marketing in bars.

The game featured four long bars, across which the bartender (you) would slide mugs of beer, ensuring that every new patron who walked in the door had suds to sip. Things escalated quickly. The more you served, the more customers would arrive demanding beer, forcing you to run from bar to bar, delivering those brews in ever-more-rapid succession. Those guests were pretty damned thirsty, as they'd chug their drinks in about one second's time and slide their mugs back for refills. It was on you to catch those empty glasses, lest they plummet to the floor and shatter. And, as these shenanigans played out, a large Budweiser logo loomed over this 16-bit bar to to remind you that you are but a cog in the wheel of consumerism.

Photo Credit: Jeff Cioletti (special thanks to the 1Up, Denver)

Naturally, a beer-themed videogame would not fly in the kiddie arcades (though it was okay in those days to leave us grade-schoolers without adult supervision in a place where half of the older regulars surely would end up on sex-offender registries). So, *Tapper* became *Root Beer Tapper* and us young'uns were none the wiser (though some local pizza and hot dog joints had the original. They must've fallen off of a truck). I remember having played *Tapper* at least as many times as I played *Root Beer Tapper*. So, the venues certainly weren't shielding this twelve-year-old's eyes from the devastatingly corrupting influence of alcohol. Come on, this was only a couple of years before Bud Light's mascot was a party-loving bull terrier whose image was on T-shirts they were selling in the kids' section of Macy's. I know this because I owned one!

Anyway, the joke was on the regulatory powers that be because many of us young, Gen X, quarter-slinging arcade rats grew up to be avid beer drinkers—with intense nostalgic streaks. Video game technology and aesthetics advanced exponentially between the 1980s and the early 2000s. Many of us embraced the Halos, Grand Theft Autos, and Call of Duties of the world, but we maintained a soft spot for all things *Pac-Man*, *Galaga*, and *Asteroids*.

When I got married, I gifted all of my groomsmen plug-and-play video game systems shaped like Atari 2600 joysticks, each containing multiple early '80s classics that were once only available on those cumbersome plastic cartridges.

Not long after that, we were getting our pixels-and-pints fix at Barcade, the craft beer and throwback videogame bars where twenty-five cents still gets you a round of *Space Invaders*. The first Barcade opened in Williamsburg, Brooklyn, in 2004 and then expanded in 2011 to my neck of the woods, Jersey City,

New Jersey. Over the next several years, Barcades opened in Manhattan, Newark, Philadelphia, and New Haven. By the time you read this, several more likely will have arrived in hip neighborhoods in other parts of the country.

Photo Credit: Jeff Cioletti (special thanks to the 1Up, Denver)

While the name Barcade has been successfully trademarked, the concept has not. And that's a lucky break for the team behind the Barcade empire because, technically, Portland, Oregon's Ground Kontrol deserves most of the credit for creating it a good five years before the Brooklyn Barcade opened its doors.

Ground Kontrol is a Portland institution with more than 150 games, including more than forty pinball machines, spread across multiple stories. It caters to the nostalgia-minded, with a classic section featuring all of the types of games you'd find at Barcade, but its selection extends into the modern era as well. And even though it's in the craft beer capital of the United States, its beer selection isn't craft-exclusive, like the East Coast arcade bar. It's actually a popular party spot with live music and DJs.

The mountain time zone also has its own mecca of 16-bit mayhem in the form of the Denver watering hole, the 1up, whose first location opened in the city's LoDo neighborhood about a month before Barcade's second spot—Jersey City—flipped the power switch. The 1up makes no secret of its inspiration. Its website notes that it loves to give credit where credit is due, specifically to Ground Kontrol and the Brooklyn Barcade. The concept was, however, new to Denver. Less than fifteen months after the LoDo location's March 2011 grand opening, the 1up cut the ribbon on its second site in the city's Capitol Hill district. The sprawling, latter location is worth the trip for the "world's largest Pac-Man" alone. Not sure if that's true, but it certainly is impressive—a floor-to-ceiling screen where the ghosts are big enough to be truly terrifying. And the console has a pair of cup holders to enable you to drown your sorrows as you're murdered by primary-color apparitions in front of everyone else in the room.

The videogame-watering hole concept isn't an entirely American phenomenon. I visited a popular cocktail bar in Gdańsk, Poland called Pixel, whose name is a not-so-subtle homage to the arcade world. If that wasn't convincing enough, its logo is an 8-bit, *Space Invaders*-style alien. The place really was a den of overall geekery, with hand-drawn Marvel and DC heroes all over the walls.

But where the Barcades, 1ups, and Ground Kontrols of the world exist to trigger our nostalgia for the quarter-popping outings of our youth, Pixel's mission is to make guests feel more at home—as if in their living rooms, on their couches. Instead of arcade-sized games, Pixel offers its visitors consoles on which to play as they sip the latest innovations in craft mixology that the talented bartenders whipped up. The craft cocktail movement started in the UK and the US, but most of Europe and the rest of the world caught up pretty quickly.

ADULTING IN THE TWENTY-FIRST CENTURY

Arcade bars have been successful in connecting us with our youth, but they have ultimately underlined a truth that's been apparent for quite some time: *videogames aren't just for kids*. Back in the '80s, we had our giant gorillas facing off against Italian stereotypes and pie-shaped yellow heads chomping at dots while evading multi-colored ghosts, but something weird happened among those of us who grew up in that era. We refused to stop playing, and the games decided to grow up with us.

Since I've always been more of a classic arcade game guy, I decided to consult with some friends who are both extremely avid gamers and, as fate would have it, longtime creative pros at major game companies.

"I think it's just accepted that it's not a kid's thing," says my friend, Laura De Young, who is head of the art department at one of the top developers in the world. Subtitles would have been helpful during our conversations; let's just say I got a crash course in gamer lingo circa 2020.

"You think about the graphics of the old games and they had this more cartoony, childlike, colorful look, and then there was this whole move to gritty, dark, super-saturated games with the Xbox 360. We went to a really dark side, with games having really mature themes like World War II," Laura observes. "It feels like an adult world. I don't know if anyone would've ever accepted Mario getting drunk."

(That may be so, but do we really know what those pills were that Pac-Man was popping?)

If the games were going to be geared toward a more mature audience, they were going to be adult enough for booze. And the libations are really flowing in many of the top modern video game franchises. The fantasy genre, like fantasy fiction, can get quite creative with the strong liquids. They absolutely have to, especially in the high-stakes world of Massively Multiplayer Online (MMO) gaming. Unforgiving barely begins to describe the rigorous, seemingly never-ending, multi-level adventures that take a toll on both the players and the characters. Sometimes those characters just need a drink. (The players will have to fend for themselves in the real world.)

"You go out in the [game's] world, there's all this shit going down, you have what they call a PUG—a pick-up group, where you're playing with strangers, sometimes four or five of you, and people are arguing," Laura explains. "Some nights you end and you're, like, 'wow, what a great night!' and some nights you end and it's like 'this sucked.' "

She developed a regular ritual for the wind down portion of the evening: Her characters in *World of Warcraft* and *EverQuest* would retire to taverns when it was time to log off. "I would always bring my character inside, grab a drink—elves usually drank some kind of dew—and then go to bed," she recalls. "I wouldn't have a drink for myself in reality, but I had a drink for my character."

And then there's *The Witcher 3*, which contributed one of the most epic drunk sequences in all of gaming. Even if you're not that into gaming, do yourself a favor and search "Witcher 3 drunk" on YouTube, and you'll likely come across the most entertaining thirteen minutes you've likely seen in the virtual world. Sorceress Yennefer has gone to sleep, leaving lead protagonist Geralt and his fellow witchers, Lambert and Eskel, to get tanked in a tavern. The three get progressively more inebriated and their speech gets increasingly slurred from copious amounts of vodka and a concoction called the gauntlet: equal parts spirit and an alchemical, hallucinogenic potion known as White Gull. We're treated to a medieval version of the "I never" drinking game, where one person says "I never did X" and those who have done that thing must drink. Lambert says he's never slept with a succubus, but we quickly learn he is unique among the trio in that regard. ("I'm a sucker for women with horns," Eskel admits). We also get a couple of tipsy "I love you, man" moments, some catty gossiping when one of the three is out of earshot, and a "drunk friend inexplicably wandering off" situation. (Eskel passes out in the snow next to a goat.) You know, like any modern night out of drinking.

The action culminates with Lambert's half-baked idea to summon a sorceress. It's the thirteenth-century equivalent of the late-night "you up?" drunk text. But then Eskel fears they might scare off the summoned one when she realizes the summoners aren't sorceresses (or "sorceressweses" in Eskel drunk-speak) themselves. Lambert suggests a solution: put on Yennefer's clothes. Nothing quite goes as planned and the moral of the story is don't drink and summon.

"I think it's actually the best drunk sequence ever made in a game," Laura says. "It absolutely captured the feeling of going out and drinking with your friends."

Game developers have gone out of their way to simulate the drinking experience with everything from shaky, blurry screens to slurred speech. For instance, you might think you're texting your fellow players, "Hey, what an epic battle that was!" but it manifests itself on screen as "bluurrbh blug bloob." Go home, elf; you're drunk.

Beyond the comical elements of inebriation, excessive drinking has some very real consequences (in the very fake world, that is).

Of all the scenarios that Laura wanted to relay to me, she had me at "forty-five-minute corpse retrieval." (I've got dibs on that name if I ever start a band.)

She and a friend were playing *EverQuest* and spent three-quarters of an hour in their ghostly forms trying to recover their corporeal selves. And why? Because drinking. "We wanted to go to this town called Freeport, which was a higher level than we were," she remembers. "We were like, 'no, no, no we want to get there. We don't care if we're just babies—we're going to go to Freeport!' "

When they finally made it to the docks, they realized they had just missed the Freeport-bound boat—which departs at forty-five-minute intervals. That meant they had to wait forty-five real-world minutes before the next ferry arrived. They didn't want to leave the dock because they thought it was a safe space, secure from all the higher-level obstacles and shenanigans that surrounded them that very likely would kill them. "We were really high up above the water, so I just said, 'let's just hang out and sit on the dock, and why don't we start drinking this mead that we've been carrying around,' " Laura explains. "This is the character that I used to get drunk with, and I've got lots of alcohol." The whole screen became a blur and they started texting each other gibberish. Now, remember, these are game characters I'm talking about. The players are stone-cold sober. It's the ones and zeroes that are hammered.

"You've got to understand how costly this whole thing is," she tells me, explaining that when you die in *EverQuest*, you lose experience. That was especially common in the earlier days of MMO, the early 2000s, *EverQuest*'s heyday. "Let's say you get to level 11, you'd go back to level 10. It takes months to max level your character. It's a really, really hard game." At the time, MMOs were rife with KOS (kill on sight) incidents. If your character reached a certain realm, you would be visible to anyone, anywhere and highly vulnerable.

So, you can see just how unfortunate what happened next was.

"I still don't know what the fuck it was," she says, "but this thing comes charging up out of the water and shot me and my friend." So, it was time for the corpse retrieval, which was incredibly complicated in its own right. "They used to call it binding, where you bound the soul of your character to a particular inn, in some particular town, in some particular spot," she explains. "We had to run across the continent in ghost form for anywhere from forty-five minutes to an hour—it's this forever run. And the problem is that when you get there, this thing that killed you is probably waiting to kill you again." And all this because they decided to get drunk on a dock to pass the time. Remember kids: *drink responsibly*. Moderation is thy master.

PLAYING IN THE SANDBOX

It's important to remember that video games, at their core, are fantasies. The real world can suck a great deal and sometimes a person just wants to escape to a plane of existence where the same rules don't apply. That's precisely why sandbox-style franchises—open-world games where players essentially can bend much of reality to their will—are so appealing. Things can get very dark pretty quickly and there are no real-world consequences. Why else do you think that the mother-of-all sandbox series, Rockstar Games's *Grand Theft Auto*, is such a household name? Even folks who've never touch a game controller in their lives know of it. A straight-laced, upstanding citizen can indulge in the taboo. If you're seventeen years old—the minimum age to purchase M-rated games, but let's be honest, kids much younger are playing it—what's more taboo than getting drunk, stealing a car, and murdering someone? Forget about the felonies for a second. If you're in your late teens, you can't buy booze. But in the *GTA* realm, the world is your liquor store. Carding be damned!

In a lot of ways, *GTA* owes a debt of gratitude to proto-sandbox sensation, *Leisure Suit Larry*, which debuted a full decade before gamers started living out their car thievery and homicide-related fantasies.

"*Leisure Suit Larry* was pretty much the childhood fantasy of what it is to be a renegade grown-up," says Robin Maddock, who played Larry in his youth and grew up to be a game designer, programmer and engineer. "It was like a kid's version of jokes. [Larry] would find some condoms somewhere and try to pick up a prostitute—and he doesn't—and then he'll get drunk and something will happen and he'd just stumble through the whole game. But it was definitely the first game that I can think of that started playing with those themes. I think I played it when I was fourteen, so it was slightly naughty."

It's no surprise that *Leisure Suit Larry* first arrived on the scene in 1987—the whole thing plays out like an '80s sex comedy.

The gaming industry tried to apply a rudimentary sort of age gate to Larry's exploits by quizzing prospective players on subjects the creators thought only grown-ups would know—like details of an episode from the early days of *Saturday Night Live*, a frame of reference the game creators didn't think late-'80s youth had. It was multiple choice and an easy system to game, even before there was such thing as a search engine to consult.

Years later, by the time Bethesda's post-apocalyptic, retro-futuristic Fallout franchise (think '50s sci-fi) became popular, alcoholic drinks became characters in their own right. Gamma Gulp beer, Bobrov's Best moonshine, Wasteland tequila, Dixon's whiskey, and the mixed drinks called the Dirty Wastelander and Nuka and Rum (a post-nuclear rum & Coke) are all familiar to Fallout devotees.

The humor's dark in an end-of-days kind of way—exactly what you'd need to survive the wasteland.

NUKA DARK RUM

The tongue-in-cheek booze of the Fallout world jumped off the screen and into our hands with the promotional release of Nuka Dark Rum. Bethesda teamed with Silver Screen Bottling Company to produce the 35 percent ABV rum liqueur, packaged in a black bottle that resembles a bomb, mimicking Nuka Cola's virtual vessel in the Fallout universe. It was launched to coincide with the November 2018 release of *Fallout 76*. The Nuka Cola Company calls it "the most refreshing way to unwind."

Of course, there was a huge waiting list for the drink and it pretty much disappeared before it even hit stores. You can find it sold by online retailers for about eighty dollars per 750-ml bottle. The liquid may not be world-class stuff, but the bottle is cool. And we all know that's the real reason anyone's buying it anyway.

It wasn't the first time such a drink entered our realm. In 2015, Carlsberg UK—the British unit of the Danish brewing giant—released Fallout Beer. Of course, it was a limited-time-only release and UK consumers won't likely find it in traditional channels anymore. However, I have seen it on eBay for two hundred dollars a case as recently as 2019. I can't vouch for its quality. It's in a green bottle, which lets in a lot of light. It's probably skunked to high heaven.

CLASSIC GAME COCKTAILS

Old school video game fans will appreciate this trio of cocktails crafted at Ground Kontrol Classic Arcade in Portland, Oregon.

PRINCESS PEACH

Mario's favorite royal inspired this one, which Ground Kontrol promotions director Dylan Snow says has been the arcade bar's most popular drink for the past few years.

- 1oz Blueberry Stoli Vodka
- 1oz peach schnapps
- 14oz hard apple cider

Stir all ingredients together in a cocktail tin and serve in a pint glass.

CUBE Q*UENCHER

Ground Kontrol bartender Kassandra Halloran developed this tequila-centric Q*bert-themed concoction.

- 1.5 ounces El Jimador Reposado tequila (or equivalent)
- Cock 'n Bull Ginger Beer
- Orange juice
- Grand Marnier float

Fill a highball glass with ice, then pour in the tequila. Pour the ginger beer to the halfway mark, followed by the orange juice nearly to the top. Float the Grand Marnier.

Photo Credit: Dylan Snow, Ground Control

DIDDY COLADA

The credit goes to Aeden McRea, who put this on Ground Kontrol's menu. The Diddy in question here is not the iconic music mogul, but Diddy Kong, who debuted in the Donkey Kong/Mario franchise back in the '90s.

- Pint glass
- 1.5oz Malibu Rum over rocks
- Coconut Red Bull
- Pineapple juice
- Myers's dark rum
- Splash of lime
- Cherry (garnish)

Fill a pint glass with ice and pour in the Malibu. Fill halfway with Coconut Red Bull; then fill to nearly the top with the pineapple juice. Float with the Myers's, add a splash of lime, and garnish with lime and cherry.

Photo Credit: Dylan Snow, Ground Control

CHAPTER 9

SHAKE THIS, 007

"You're doing it wrong."

I generally hate the click-baity articles that pedantically try to tell readers that they've been performing such-and-such task, eating such-and-such meal, or drinking such-and-such beverage incorrectly their entire lives. But I give a pass to the plethora of online items written to let us know that James Bond really doesn't know how to order a martini.

Let's start with the obvious. Traditionally, before James Bond's time, martinis had been made with gin, period. Having said that, the classic drink's history wasn't exactly etched in stone. There are a lot of conflicting theories related to the martini's origin story. One of those is that it evolved from the Martinez, a mid-to-late-nineteenth-century concoction made with Old Tom gin—a sweeter variety than the now-dominant London dry style—vermouth, maraschino liqueur, bitters, and a slice of lemon. There's also a very good chance that the original ingredient wasn't technically gin at all, but gin's Dutch forerunner, Jenever. The key difference between gin and Jenever is the latter's concentration of what's known as "malt wine"—not wine at all, but a grain spirit that's essentially a rudimentary whiskey. What we know today as gin, on the other hand, has a neutral spirit base. All of gin's flavor comes from the botanicals, of which juniper is the prevailing influence. Jenever has juniper, as well as other botanicals, but there's more balance between the flavor of the infused or re-distilled flora and the base grain distillate.

Photo Credit: Craige Moore

At the approximate time of the Martinez's invention, Jenever was being imported in significant quantities to the US. Hence, there's a good case to be made for its presence in the cocktail's earliest iterations.

Origin stories aside, gin was the spirit of choice in the martini's heyday, long before vodka was really even a thing in the US.

One of my favorite bars in the United States is the Gin Joint in Charleston, South Carolina. For a while, the Gin Joint had prided itself on mixing its drinks with spirits that were around before, immediately after, and during Prohibition. That's why you wouldn't find vodka on the menu.

But around the time the Ian Fleming wrote *Casino Royale* in 1952, vodka had come into vogue in the United Kingdom and had also made its way to the US. Its neutrality was its appeal. It was eminently mixable, never competing with or overpowering a drink's other ingredients. It was the perfect alcohol delivery system. It just didn't have any of its own character. Bond essentially was drinking diluted ethanol with the subtle flavor of dry vermouth and the mere suggestion of citrus.

In Bond's first on-screen outing, *Dr. No*, there's no mistaking what's in his glass. When the titular villain presents Bond with his drink at the former's oceanic HQ, Dr. No identifies it as a "dry martini, lemon peel, shaken, not stirred." Bond asks, "Vodka?" to which Dr. No replies, "of course." It's as if gin was never even part of the equation.

And then there's that whole "shaken, not stirred" notion.

A martini, like all spirit-heavy mixed drinks, should always be stirred. Shaking is for cocktails that include citrus juices and egg whites—the latter of which are used to create a foamy consistency.

Therefore, it's not entirely unfair to say James Bond ruined the martini, but you can't blame Ian Fleming and film producer Albert Broccoli for not letting tradition get in the way of a good catch phrase. The phrase first appeared in the mid-'50s novel *Diamonds Are Forever*. Though he did order a shaken martini in the first Bond novel, *Casino Royale*, he didn't follow up his request with "…not stirred." Bond didn't actually utter "shaken, not stirred" himself until he officially made the jump from page to screen in *Dr. No*. So, you really need to give credit to both the book series' author and the filmmakers.

With so much focus on the martini, you'd think that is all 007 ever drinks. Sure, he has one in the majority of the movies that have been made thus far, but he also has a "when in Rome" attitude when it comes to the local beverages in various parts of the world. And he travels *a lot*.

"What we love about these movies is not only are they snapshots of places, they're also snapshots of time," says Craig Ormiston, who, along with his friend Eddy Colloton, created Licence to Drink, a blog, cocktail series, and monthly themed party built around the James Bond universe. The site and Instagram account showcase drinks they've devised, along with newer co-conspirator Kierra Aiello, inspired by the Ian Fleming books and the movies.

"James Bond is a fairly learned and worldly character," Ormiston adds. "He knows what to drink and where, and if he doesn't, he tends to know something about it if it's exposed to him."

Colloton notes that, especially in the earlier Connery films, the movies—and their requisite drinks—were more in the spirit of the original Fleming novels. "They're kind of travelogue-y and say something about where the movie takes place or who the characters are whom he's meeting with," Colloton says.

I want to talk about some of the unsung boozes that appeared on screen in the Bond universe over the course of nearly six decades.

ICONIC CONNERY

Dr. No

As much of the action of this film takes place in Jamaica, it's no surprise that there was some fairly clever product placement for the island nation's biggest beer brand, Red Stripe.

In an early scene, Bond gets into a bit of a hand-to-hand situation with Quarrel and bar owner Puss-Feller, and he ultimately kicks and throws both of them into a stack of (very obviously empty) Red Stripe cases—before he knows they are allies, of course.

But that wasn't the Jamaican brew's first appearance in the Bond-iverse. Its first mentions were in print—in the *Dr. No* source novel, as well as the book version of *The Man with the Golden Gun*, which would find its way to the screen with Roger Moore (and the legendary Christopher Lee, I might add) in 1974.

Dr. No is also notable as not only the first Bond movie, but the one in which the filmmakers establish the rare, committed 007 love affair—not with a woman, but with Dom Pérignon.

The legendary champagne makes numerous appearances throughout the film and book series. Interestingly, the preferred vintage tends to vary. In *Dr. No*, Bond says he prefers the '53 (after the titular baddie says, "That's a Dom Perignon '55. It would be a pity to break it.")

From Russia with Love

"Ah, raki. Filthy stuff," says Bond's Istanbul contact Kerim Bey in what likely was English-speaking movie audiences' first introduction to Turkey's traditional aniseed spirit. Still, he and Bond both partook when they arrived at a dinner with Kerim Bey's allies.

After one of the most misogynistic sequences in a franchise rife with misogynistic sequences (a physical altercation between two women over a man, a gratuitous "catfight"), and an assassination-attempt-turned-shoot-out with a cadre of armed assailants, Bond declares, "I'll take care of this filthy stuff," and proceeds to drink the remaining raki right from the bottle. "Filthy" is quite unfair. When made well, raki can be quite elegant.

Goldfinger

Bond and M meet with Colonel Smithers from the Bank of England to discuss the titular villain's potentially illegal gold smuggling operation. Naturally, they do so over some fancy drinks. "Have a little more of this rather disappointing brandy," Smithers says. "What's wrong with it," M inquires. Bond, who never misses an opportunity to show how much of a cultured know-it-all he is, interjects with, "I'd say it was a thirty-year-old fined, indifferently blended, with an overdose of Bon Bois."

M is all of us, shutting down an insufferable booze snob, when he replies, "Colonel Smithers is giving the lecture, 007!" Bon Bois, incidentally, is a region within Cognac known for its soils rich in lime and clay, producing distinctive grapes that ultimately get distilled into Cognac. It translates directly to "good wood," once again proving that everything sounds exponentially fancier in French. (A missed opportunity for a double entendre, I might add.)

Much later in the film, when Bond is being held against his will at Goldfinger's Kentucky stud farm, Goldfinger, ever the hospitable host, offers 007 a mint julep—it *is* bourbon country after all. However, I will never get used to seeing the drink in a tall Collins glass. Yes, I know plenty of places serve it that way. The classic shiny cup would have been much more aesthetically pleasing on film—especially if the iconic villain had bespoke versions made with his favorite precious metal instead of the traditional silver. Another bone I have to pick with Bond is that he asked for his julep to contain "some ice." In my opinion, it's not a julep if it doesn't have *a lot* of ice. I like it when it's essentially a bourbon-sugar-and-mint snow cone.

Thunderball

The 1965 release is the first of what I like to call the "Dom Pérignon trilogy." Immediately after Bond defeats villain Emilio Largo in a card game in Nassau, 007 shares some beluga caviar and a bottle of Dom Pérignon '55 with Largo's mistress, Domino. He's obviously trying to impress her (it works). A bit later we get a touch of product placement foreshadowing when the umbrellas at a Bahamian street market advertise Amstel beer. Forty-seven years later, at the pinnacle of the Daniel Craig era, Heineken becomes Bond's brew of choice in *Skyfall*.

Heineken International acquired Amstel about three years after *Thunderball* first hit screens.

This being the Caribbean and all, it was only a matter of time before rum came into the picture. When 007 visits Palmyra, Largo's island lair, he indulges in a Rum Collins (a molasses-based riff on the classic Tom Collins) to fuel up for an afternoon of skeet shooting. Later, a bottle of the spirit comes in handy as an incendiary device.

You Only Live Twice

There's a lot to be annoyed with in the Japan-set adventure—the one where we finally get to see Ernst Stavro Blofeld's face (not that it matters because it's the only time he's played by Donald Pleasence).

Early in the film, when Bond breaks into Osato Chemical (whose principal is in league with SPECTRE) and subsequently subdues a heavy, he takes a drink of whatever bottle is at his disposal. In this case, it's "Siamese vodka"—and 007 is vocal about his displeasure at the existence of such a thing. Mr. Bond, you fancy yourself a connoisseur of the finer things and, yet in your mind, vodka should come from Russia (with love!) or Poland. Granted, vodka was still relatively new to palates outside the Iron Curtain in the '60s, so some people can be forgiven their purism, but "vodka" is not a protected appellation. It can be distilled anywhere in the world and called such. The spirit is supposed to be neutral in flavor, color, and aroma—characteristics that any distiller on any continent can achieve with some good technical know-how. And that includes Thailand, the country formerly known as Siam.

But the bigger head-scratcher is the inevitable sake scene (this is Japan, after all). When Bond's Japanese intelligence liaison, Tiger Tanaka presents 007 with the fermented rice beverage and asks him if he likes it, the British secret agent responds that he indeed does, "especially when it's served at the correct temperature, 98.4 degrees Fahrenheit, like this." So much to unpack with that statement!

Before I do, let me qualify my commentary with the fact that I'm basing it on modern sake standards, which have changed somewhat dramatically since 1967, the year of this film's release. Very few styles were available to Western consumers at the time. Still, I had mixed feelings when I revisited *You Only Live Twice* as a newly minted International Kikisake-shi (a sake sommelier, just a lot more fun to say). While a temperature two-tenths of a point cooler than that of the human body is perfectly acceptable for some sake, it's hardly "correct" for every bottle under the sun. Even the most heat-friendly sake should be warmed to no more than 131 degrees Fahrenheit (55 degrees Celsius, which is considered "very hot" in sake lingo). Bond's "correct" temperature is between what's now known as "lukewarm" (95 degrees Fahrenheit, 35 degrees Celsius) and "low warm" (104 degrees Fahrenheit, 40 degrees Celsius). There are nine such temperature designations in modern sake classification, but let's not go down that rabbit hole. Incidentally, Osato's office is the venue for the latest Dom Pérignon sighting. This time it's a '59.

THE LAZENBY LAYOVER

On Her Majesty's Secret Service

OHMSS had been, for the longest time, my favorite Bond film, only to be knocked off its throne by *Skyfall* in 2015. (George

Lazenby, however, was my least favorite Bond. I dare to dream how much better *OHMSS* could have been had Connery not taken a powder.) The movie also manages to succeed despite a tragically miscast Telly Savalas as Blofeld (complete with Queens, New York accent), replacing the far-superior Donald Pleasence as the villain. It can be seen as the first Bond "epic." No less epic is the list of boozes that are name checked throughout the nearly two-and-a-half-hour motion picture.

Deo Optimo Maximo makes its final appearance in the 1960s Bond film, this time as the '57 vintage. The bubbly shows up early in the film when 007 shares his first drink with Tracy (Diana Rigg, *The Avengers'* Emma Peel herself), the woman who would become, *spoiler alert*, the ill-fated Mrs. Bond. (As polarizing a notion that a married—albeit very briefly—Bond is for most fans, the wedding scene at the tail end of *OHMSS* is one the best moments in the entire franchise. It's a real "family" moment, with M, Q, and Moneypenny interacting in a social setting.)

When 007 meets Tracy's dad, Draco, the construction magnate and gangster offers Bond his usual shaken-not-stirred sipper, while Draco indulges in a rather generous pour of Campari in a sizeable goblet. The bitter liqueur is usually close to 30 percent alcohol and Draco was drinking at least eight ounces of it. Do the math!

Apparently, as Bond points out, Campari's not even Draco's signature tipple. That would be Corsican brandy. I'd like to think that that's some sort of exotic eau-de-vie distilled from an ingredient indigenous to Corsica like chestnuts, but it's very likely a barrel-aged brandy made from one of many of the French-speaking island's wine grape varietals. That's not to say chestnut brandy isn't a thing—it's very much an island specialty, typically consumed as a digestive.

In the middle of the film's second act, when Bond impersonates genealogist Sir Hilary Bray to infiltrate Blofeld's mountaintop "clinic," he order's Bray's go-to drink, "malt whiskey and branch water." There's about a 99.9 percent chance that it's Scotch whisky he's drinking because Irish whiskeys tend to have some unmalted grain in them. And, at the time, Irish whiskey was struggling with a crisis of reputation (no longer, thankfully), so someone as cultured as Sir Hilary probably would have considered it slumming to indulge in Ireland's grain spirit. Now, about that "branch water." It's just a fancy name for fresh water, pulled from a stream or other pristine source without any chemical adulteration.

Immediately after the climactic Bond-versus-Blofeld bobsled smackdown (spoiler alert: 007 wins), a St. Bernard greets a weary 007 with some affectionate licks. "Never mind that," snaps Bond. "Go get the brandy. Five-star Hennessy, of course." The whole St. Bernard with a brandy-barrel-collar thing is supposedly a myth. And even if it weren't, it's doubtful the dog handlers would spring for Cognac. Personally, I think the line should have been, "Never mind that. Go get Donald Pleasence back."

ONE MORE FOR THE ROAD FOR CONNERY

Diamonds Are Forever

The one-and-done Lazenby never really had the chance to settle into the 007 role. Thankfully, Connery came back for one last go-round—a dozen years before he'd don the tuxedo once more in the unofficial Bond entry, *Never Say Never Again*, during the waning days of Roger Moore's tenure. Not-so-thankfully,

Diamonds Are Forever was, by far, the weakest of the Connery oeuvre. The B-movie-level special effects (reportedly due to the fact that Connery's salary ate up much of the budget), a preposterous reveal involving Blofeld doppelgangers and a space laser, the ridiculously campy henchmen Mr. Wint and Mr. Kidd (who would've seemed more at home battling Adam West's Batman than 007), and centerfold-ready bodyguards Bambi and Thumper are only a few of this mess of a movie's problems. And it certainly doesn't help that yet another actor (Charles Gray) is playing Blofeld with yet another inconsistent accent (this time posh English) and an inexplicably full head of hair. It's like they weren't even trying.

Having said all that, *Diamonds Are Forever* boasts one of the best boozy moments in the entire film series thus far.

In the requisite expositional information dump early in the movie, Diamond Syndicate chairman Sir Donald Munger offers 007 and M some sherry. M declines, citing "doctor's orders."

"Pity about your liver, sir," Bond replies. "It's an unusually fine solera. '51, I believe."

A clearly exasperated M snaps back: "There is no year for sherry, 007."

It's, perhaps, the clearest indication yet, that Bond's boss finds the agent's snobbish showboating to be quite insufferable. Unfortunately, M was a bit hasty in calling out 007's faux pas, for it was not a faux pas at all.

"I was referring to the original vintage on which the sherry is based, sir—1851," Bond retorts. "It's unmistakable."

Sir Donald confirms that Bond is correct.

Sherry, the fortified wine made in the Spanish city of Jerez, is aged in oak casks through the solera method, whereby a fraction of a liquid from a barrel whose contents are of a certain age is blended with similarly small portions of wines of a range of ages. The barrels are stacked on top of each other, with the oldest on the bottom and the youngest on top.

Sherry is fortified with a bit of spirit, which ups the alcohol percentage a few points. The finished product is usually around 19 percent ABV, compared to about 13 percent for regular, un-fortified wine.

When the conversation turns to diamonds, 007 admits that his familiarity with the precious stones is quite average: "Hardest substance found in nature, they cut glass, they suggest marriage. I suppose they replaced a dog as a girl's best friend. That's about it."

"Refreshing to hear there's one subject you're not an expert on," M responds, in a cheer-worthy epic burn.

MOORE, PLEASE

Live and Let Die

The first of seven Roger Moore films in what would be a twelve-year tenure is a bit of a mixed bag. There's the obvious attempt at "blaxploitation," one of many zeitgeist-y maneuvers the franchise employs over the next decade or so to maintain its relevance. (Frankly, it comes off as more cringe-worthy and racist. The scene where Sheriff J.W. Pepper—supposedly the comic-relief character—pulls a stop-and-frisk on one of the black antagonists and addresses him as "boy" is skin crawling.)

But then there is, arguably, one of the best Bond theme songs. The titular number by Paul McCartney and Wings is no less iconic than Shirley Bassey's ode to the eponymous Big Bad in *Goldfinger.* (And, it's McCartney's best post-Beatles tune to date.) And there is one noteworthy booze-related moment in Moore's debut. When 007 meets Felix Leiter in a bar in New Orleans, the CIA agent encourages Bond to "live a little" and get the classic Big Easy cocktail, the Sazerac—traditionally rye whiskey, absinthe, bitters, sugar, and lemon peel. It was almost as though 007 forgot who he was for a moment (and to be fair, this is the first time with the new face) and was about to neglect drinking as the locals drink.

The Man with the Golden Gun

This one gets a bit of a bad rap—its underwhelming box office and not-so-stellar reviews nearly torpedoed the franchise for good—but I think there's much to like about Roger Moore's second outing (the usual bikini-clad misogyny notwithstanding). Francisco Scaramanga is vastly underrated among Bond villains. Christopher Lee's performance makes him likeable and terrifying at the same time.

The Man with the Golden Gun is also the film where Bond's snobbery gets called out again—not by his boss this time, but by the audience. While enjoying a cozy dinner with Mary Goodnight (Britt Ekland) in Bangkok, the waiter delivers a bottle of local wine to the table. "Phu Yuck?!" Bond exclaims, as if someone has just urinated in his beluga caviar.

It's a rare fish-out-of-water moment for a secret agent who easily glides in and out of local customs, no matter where he is.

"Seventy-four, sir," the server informs him. I'm not sure if that in itself was supposed to be a joke, because 1974 was the year the film was released and it's unlikely that it was any sort of vintage. (He does seem pleasantly surprised when he sips it, unless that's just his Casino Royale poker face). It doesn't matter either way. Phu Yuck not a real brand. At least no winery had to be offended.

What is a real brand, however, is Dom Pérignon, which makes its latest Bond universe cameo in this movie. This time it's at Scaramanga's private island when the million-bucks-a-kill assassin's right-hand man, Nick Nack (Hervé Villechaize, pre-*Fantasy Island*) offers 007 a bit of hospitality in the form of "Dom Pérignon soixante-quatre" ('64). "I prefer the '62 myself." Half the time, I wonder if he even knows what he's talking about because his favorite vintage changes with each film. Then again, the actor who plays him changes pretty frequently, too, so I'll cut him some slack.

For Scaramanga, the presentation was more about showing off his skills than it was being a good host. With his titular weapon of choice, he shot off the cork from quite a distance. Even Bond's not that smooth.

The Spy Who Loved Me

Nearly three years passed between the release of *The Man with the Golden Gun* and *The Spy Who Loved Me* (see "nearly torpedoed the franchise" above), but the time away did the series some good. The *Spy Who Loved Me* ranks as my second-favorite Roger Moore flick, for what it's worth. Despite the globe-trotting from Egypt to Sardinia, to the middle of the ocean and beyond, we don't get any guest appearances by too many exotic international spirits. There is one brief, amusing moment when 007 and his Soviet rival Major Anya Amasova a.k.a. Agent XXX (Barbara Bach) are demonstrating how well they know each other's habits by ordering their respective drinks. "The Lady will have Bacardi on the rocks," Bond says.

"And the gentleman," Amasova adds, "vodka martini, shaken, not stirred."

I love the "booze badge" aspect of this scene. I'm a strong proponent of getting out of one's comfort zone and trying new drinks whenever one can, but it's more than fine to return home to our old standbys—the drinks the define us—from time to time. A vodka martini is Bond's badge, just as the world's number one rum brand over ice is Agent XXX's.

There's an interesting side note about Amasova's chosen beverage. She's a true believer in communist ideology, but the Bacardi family is not. Even though the members of the Cuban founding family were friends with Castro prior to his revolution, their feelings for him soured once his regime seized all private property. Luckily, they already had operations in Puerto Rico, where they consolidated all of their distilling operations after they fled Cuba. Could that be Amasova offering a quiet, subversive nod of solidarity with the Bacardi family, or is she intentionally pouring salt on their wounds? We may never know.

But what we do know is that Dom makes another cameo—this time the '52 as the two spies from either side of the Iron Curtain flee Stromberg's exploding underwater city in his luxurious escape pod (which he doesn't need because he's dead).

Moonraker

Bond leans into the whole sci-fi thing. Bit of trivia here: At the end of *Spy Who Loved Me*, the title card reads "James Bond Will Return in *For Your Eyes Only*." While this was technically true, it was a bit premature. The producers had every intention of making *For Your Eyes Only* the next film to hit theaters, but the overwhelming, unexpected success of *Star Wars*—released a little more than two months before *The Spy Who Loved Me*—prompted EON Productions to change course and fast-track the space movie as the next entry (though only the final act actually took place in space).

Bollinger makes a couple of appearances in *Moonraker*, once on Earth and once about one-hundred-fifty miles above the planet. The former was just an excuse to sell a cheeky Bond-ian one-liner at Dr. Holly Goodhead's (Lois Chiles) in Venice.

Dr. Goodhead: Fix yourself a drink.

Bond (noticing bottle): Bollinger. If it's '69, you were expecting me.

(Hey, I don't write this stuff. Just calling balls and strikes here.)

The second appearance is far more significant. This time it's uber-assassin Jaws (Richard Kiel), who'd just turned from the dark side. (Oh come on, if the Bond franchise can rip off *Star Wars*, so can I!) He and his new girlfriend are the last ones who remain on villain Drax's (Michael Lonsdale) space station. He finds the bottle, pops the cork, and toasts, "Well, here's to us." It's the first time the formidable giant ever speaks in the two consecutive 007 flicks in which he appears. Sadly, it's also the last, because he never appears again. I would've loved future editions in which he's on call whenever Bond needs some extra muscle.

But the space-age Bollinger moment was a great sendoff for him. The fact that Jaws is drinking one of 007's old standbys is as much a forging of an alliance with his former nemesis as it is an affectionate moment with his lady love.

For Your Eyes Only

This is actually my favorite of the Roger Moore flicks—mainly because it dialed back a bit of the campy cartoonishness of most of his movies (though, by today's standards, certainly not enough). It was a nice palate cleanser after the over-the-top sci-fi antics of *Moonraker* and *The Spy Who Loved Me*, because it lacked the comic book-style villain of either of those. I especially love the snowy Cortina sequences—not to mention the steamy, cold-weather staple of German-speaking areas: glühwein. Sure, it's Italy, but Cortina's only about forty miles from the Austrian border, so the locations get a bit blurred.

When Bond first meets Aristotle Kristatos at a table adjacent to an outdoor ice rink in Cortina, Kirstatos offers 007 a cup of the wine, which is heated with various baking spices and sometimes a shot of a distilled spirit. The scene always transports me to the Christkindlmarkts of Germany, Switzerland, and Austria—the only places where I'm happy to drink outside when it's 25 degrees Fahrenheit. And that's despite the fact that Kristatos turns out to be a bad guy. The first clue should've been that Julian Glover played the role.

The Greek aniseed spirit also makes an appearance a bit later when Bond orders it at dinner with Kristatos in Corfu, Greece a bit later in the film. (Ever the "when in Rome" sort of guy—

well, when in Corfu, in this case.) Kristatos then recommends that 007 order a glass of white Robola wine from the former's home region of Cephalonia (home of one of Greece's prized indigenous grapes) but Bond declines, noting "I find that a little too scented for my palate" and that he prefers the Theotoky Aspero.

It's one of the many moments throughout the film series when Bond weaponizes booze. It's his way of passive-aggressively saying, "Don't mess with me, I know my shit." And in this case, it was rather intuitive of him because, at that point in the film, Kristatos seemed more friend than foe.

Octopussy

If *Moonraker* was 007's *Star Wars*, *Octopussy* was its *Raiders of the Lost Ark*. The tuk tuk chase through the streets of New Delhi had a definite Indiana Jones vibe to it, as did the priceless antiquity of a Macguffin. A year later, George Lucas and Steven Spielberg seemed to return the favor with a very Bond-esque opening scene in Shanghai's Club Obi-Wan in *Indiana Jones and the Temple of Doom*.

Octopussy may have been heavy on picturesque, set-piece action sequences, but it was pretty light on the imbibing. (The eating was another story. Roasted sheep's head, anyone?) He's enjoying champagne with Octopussy henchwoman Magda during the film's first act, but there's none of the trademark 007 pretension here. Not a single brand gets name checked, so we'll have to assume it's Bond's trusty Bollinger.

At the end of the movie, when James is convalescing in the care of the titular smuggler and multi-millionaire (possibly billionaire) mogul, a bottle is chilling in an ice bucket. I'm also going with Bollinger on this one, though the vintage is anyone's guess.

A View to a Kill

After twelve years, Roger Moore finally called it quits—in rather inauspicious fashion, given the turkey that is this mid-'80s entry into the 007 pantheon. (*For Your Eyes Only* would have been a better place to stop). Having said that, I love the (fairly nonsensical) Duran Duran title number and Christopher Walken being all Christopher Walken-y as psychotic multi-billionaire Max Zorin.

Also enjoyable is the Stoli product placement during the pre-title sequence. Having successfully completed his Siberian mission (complete with impromptu snowboarding to a lackluster cover of the Beach Boys' "California Girls"), Bond escapes in a boat disguised as a small glacier, piloted by operative Kimberley Jones. He reveals to her the spoils of his mission: In addition to the microchip he was tasked with procuring, he produces a container of beluga caviar (natch) and a bottle of Stoli, which he intends to enjoy with Agent Jones on the cozy, five-day journey to Alaska. It seems quaint now, but back in those days Stoli really did represent a taste of the good life. No other widely distributed vodka brand had as much cachet at the time.

The rest of the movie is pretty standard stuff—and that means more Bollinger.

TIPPLES WITH TIMOTHY

The Living Daylights

Timothy Dalton doesn't get enough credit. He was doing the grim, serious intensity thing nearly two full decades before Daniel Craig made it his modus operandi. And, Soviet/Afghan war backdrop notwithstanding, *TLD* seems fairly timeless in comparison with much of the rest of the Bond oeuvre. Many of the cars and hairstyles—particularly Kara Milovy's (Maryam d'Abo)—are far less era-specific than those of the Connery, Moore, and Brosnan years. (The jury's still out on the Craig era.) The fact that a sizeable portion of the film was shot in the ageless city that is Vienna (even the sequences that were supposed to be Bratislava) certainly helped.

But if there's one thing that is an unmistakable facet of the Thatcher-Reagan years, it's unapologetic capitalism. While product placement had always had a home in the 007 franchise, *TLD* marks a turning point where it starts to become more and more blatant. In the pre-title sequence, when the newly minted Bond is engaged in fisticuffs in a moving truck with the mole who's been assassinating agents during a supposed training exercise, said vehicle barrels through some outdoor café umbrellas promoting J&B Blended Scotch whisky. At about the midpoint of the movie, a neon logo for Denmark's Carlsberg beer adorns the wall of the café at the amusement park where some deadly activity's about to go down.

A bit later, following Bond's phony "assassination" of General Pushkin (John Rhys-Davies), Felix Leiter, who believed the act to be real, has 007 "kidnapped" to figure out just what the hell he was thinking. When he learns the assassination was all a ruse, he breaks out a bottle of Jim Beam bourbon and two glasses.

Stoli makes another, very visible appearance when Kara fixes James's signature martini ("you remembered," he marvels) with the iconic Russian vodka brand. Of course, at this point in the film, she's misled to believe that Bond is a KGB agent in disguise and shakes, not stirs the concoction a bit further with some chloral hydrate. (I'm honestly surprised that that scenario doesn't occur more often, given the fact that virtually every operative on seven continents knows 007's favorite tipple.)

Licence to Kill

One of the more *meh* Bond films. Not bad, just *meh*. And, sadly, it was the last for Timothy Dalton, who demonstrated much more potential to become a Bond for the ages. *Meh* pretty much describes its boozy content as well. Sure, you get the token "shaken, not stirred" moment and there's the usual Bollinger shout-out (in this case, Bollinger R.D., when 007 arrives at the hotel in "Isthmus City"), but it seems like *Licence to Kill* (LTK) was more interested in kilos upon kilos of cocaine than it was alcohol. The film was kind of a missed opportunity, considering the fact that there is a pretty badass bar fight at the "Bimini Barrelhead Bar." I use quotes because the bar isn't actually in Bimini, the Bahamas; it's in Florida, where it's just "Barrelhead Bar."

Incidentally, Bimini was one of the favored haunts of Ernest Hemingway, who plays a sort of peripheral role in *LTK*. Hemingway's former Key West home makes a cameo, notably as the backdrop for Bond's famous resignation and revocation of the titular "licence." (Yes, I insist on spelling it the British way; the US distributor didn't Americanize the spelling for the film's stateside release, so I won't either.) Bond even quips, "I guess it's…a farewell to arms." When you're so overtly referencing an author who knew his way around a drink, you'd think *LTK* would make a little more effort on the liquor front.

PIERCE-ING THE ARMOR

GoldenEye

In Pierce Brosnan's inaugural outing as the world's most iconic secret agent, the first post-opening-title-sequence scene features some high-speed Aston Martin shenanigans as an MI6 shrink rides along to evaluate him. The evaluator is a young woman, so Bond's actions are more about trying to impress and woo her than anything else. (Lead actors may change, but the lead character's libido never does.) After a bit of automotive cat-and-mouse with Xenia Onatopp (Famke Janssen), 007 finally complies with the shrink's demand to stop the car. Of course, Bond has ulterior motives for doing so. He opens a secret compartment in the vehicle's console and out pops a fully chilled bottle of—yep, you guessed it—Bollinger, this time the 1988 vintage.

There's a scene a bit later in the second act where 007 sips what is very clearly Jack Daniel's with M. (It's Judi Dench's first appearance has Bond's boss. She's also the first to call Bond a "sexist misogynist," in that very same scene.) Interestingly, the biggest explosion was not on screen, but in theaters as the heads of hundreds of thousands of whiskey aficionados spontaneously combusted when M referred to the brand as "bourbon." While bourbon and Tennessee whiskey share a very similar recipe, don't ever call Jack anything but the latter. I'm not going to get into the minutiae of the "Lincoln County Process." Trust me, you'll thank me for that.

Since a good chunk of *GoldenEye* takes place in St. Petersburg, Russia, you can bet there will be a vodka sighting sooner or later. When 007 meets with KGB-agent-turned-Russian-gangster Valentin Zukovsky (Robbie Coltrane, better known to younger generations as Hagrid in the Harry Potter movies), Zukovsky pours himself a glass of Smirnoff Black, the small-batch offering from the largest vodka brand in the world. It's distilled in copper pot stills instead of continuous, column stills, as is the norm for the spirit. The process is supposed to give the vodka more character, as well as some premium, artisanal cred, but, at the end of the day, it's still vodka—a spirit that's supposed to be neutral in flavor and aroma (as well as color). Keep in mind that *GoldenEye* hit cinemas in 1995, before there was much of a "super-premium" vodka segment to speak of. Belvedere Vodka debuted only two years earlier and Grey Goose two years later. This was a time when Absolut was still considered the epitome of "fancy." So, for Zukovsky, this is a symbol of wealth and decadence—the newfound wealth of post-Soviet Russia. *GoldenEye* was the first Bond film after the fall of the Iron Curtain, and life in that new era was a major theme of the movie. Zukovsky drives that point home after he completes a business call and declares, "Free-market economy is going to be the death of me."

The Smirnoff Black moment is also a bit of a power play—an assertion of dominance by a nouveau riche mobster over the government-paycheck-cashing, Cold War relic that is James Bond. The fact that Zukovsky doesn't offer 007 a glass speaks volumes.

Tomorrow Never Dies

There's another of those "drink as identity" moments in *Tomorrow Never Dies*, a generally entertaining mess of a movie. At the gala where Bond reunites with former flame Paris Carver (Teri Hatcher), now wife of media mogul and main villain Elliot Carver (a scenery-chewing Jonathan Pryce), Paris asks the waiter to bring Bond the spy's signature martini. It's a good way to save a lot of exposition, especially when a character has as little screen time as Paris does. (Spoiler alert!) It indicates exactly how well she knows her erstwhile lover. (Of course, it was a missed opportunity to just bring back a character we'd already met in a previous adventure. I know, I know, it would be un-Bondian for a female character and actor, aside from Moneypenny, to return for another film). Bond assumes Paris will have what he remembers as her usual tipple, straight tequila, but she declines, saying she'll have some of her husband's champagne. "Moving up in the world," Bond replies. We get it, Paris, you've changed—and your husband is a super-rich Rupert-Murdoch type, not a spy on a government salary.

We do get a glimpse at 007 drinking a kind of deconstructed version of his martini—well, if you consider no vermouth, no ice, no garnish, and no martini glass to be "deconstructed." After a run in with Elliot Carver's goons, Bond nurses the pain with straight shots of Smirnoff.

The World Is Not Enough

Scotch whisky plays a pivotal role in the first act of *The World is Not Enough* and pretty much sets the entire plot in motion. Actually, it's Bond's penchant for putting ice in his whisky that enables MI6 to uncover the baddies' nefarious plans. When 007 is about to have a drink in M's office, his hand starts to foam. He realizes that it's because there is some sort of—likely explosive—chemical on the money he just retrieved for Sir Robert King. Unfortunately, he's a bit too late and the millions of pounds sterling in cash goes kerblam, taking Sir Robert with it. After a bit of expository forensics, we learn that the money was dipped in urea, which started a chemical reaction when it touched the water from the ice on Bond's hand.

We also get what, sadly, is Robbie Coltrane's final appearance as Valentin Zukovsky, as well as another glimpse at his favorite vodka, Smirnoff Black (served in the casino he now owns). And, we get another quaint Zukovsky reference to post-Soviet Russia's economic situation ("I'm a slave to the free-market economy.")

I was much more interested in the moment when the diabolical terrorist Renard (Robert Carlyle, Begbie from *Trainspotting*!) brought drinks for the crew of the submarine he was going to use to essentially blow Istanbul off the map. The booze in question was Ihlara Brendi (brandy), more or less Turkey's answer to Cognac. Naturally, the brandy was drugged, killing everyone on board. But don't let that put you off of Ihlara.

Die Another Day

We get back into the travelogue-y aspect of Bond's drinking escapades when he's in Cuba. He meets up with cigar maker and occasional secret agent Raoul to get intel on the potential whereabouts of bad guy Zao. Bond sips some sort of brown liquor. Knowing 007's tastes, I'd guess it was probably Scotch whisky. However, it's Havana, so I'd bet more money on aged rum. In the States, we still can't get much of the really good Cuban stuff. There's actually an ongoing battle over which parent company, Bacardi or Pernod Ricard, owns the country's most iconic rum brand, Havana Club. The Havana Club that we get here isn't actually made in Cuba. Much of the rest of the world gets the Havana-made stuff. It's a controversy that never seems to end.

And, speaking of rum, we get to hear Bond pronounce mojito with what he thinks is the closest thing to a Cuban accent. He does it on more than one occasion in the film and it's almost comical.

But you've got to give the writers a lot of credit here for being on trend. In 2002, the year *Die Another Day* was released, the cocktail renaissance was just starting to pick up steam. The mojito has existed in some form for centuries, but its popularity surged anew on British and American shores in the new millennium. White rum, lime juice, sugar, soda water and, of course, mint create a drink far better than the sum of its parts.

Bond's drinking a mojito the first time he meets Halle Berry's Jinx, who emerges from the surf Ursula Andress-style (it was the fortieth anniversary of the film franchise and the fiftieth anniversary of the publication of Fleming's first Bond book, so director Lee Tamahori threw in a lot of homage-y Easter eggs). He shares the minty delight with her—and shares a lot more with her that evening.

Martini alert: Bond's on the plane back to London (complete with the Clash's "London Calling" playing on the soundtrack). There's a bit of turbulence. "Lucky I asked for it shaken."

Bollinger alert: The '61, which 007 orders as he's checking into the presidential suite at the hotel in Hong Kong.

CRAIG'S LIST

Casino Royale

The first film of the Daniel Craig era had quite a bit to accomplish—perhaps more than any one cinematic Bond entry has had to pull off since *On Her Majesty's Secret Service*. Not only did it have to introduce a new lead actor—been there, done that—but it was the first official "reboot" of the franchise. For all intents and purposes, Connery, Lazenby, Moore, Dalton, and Brosnan weren't all just playing Bond; they were, ostensibly, playing the *same* Bond. (You could make a case for *GoldenEye* being that reboot. However, reboots weren't really a thing yet in the mid-'90s and you had to accept the established continuity.) But *Casino Royale* was a bona fide origin story (despite the fact that Judi Dench was reprising her role as the post-Cold War M). It also was a drastic tonal departure from the vast majority of the films that came before it. (*The Living Daylights* came relatively close, tonally.) This was a grittier, more reality-based Bond, similar to the Caped Crusader who was reinvented a year and a half before in *Batman Begins*. This 007 went out of his way to let us know that—particularly in his very first martini moment. After losing a boatload of (the British government's) cash at the titular gambling den, a clearly agitated Bond goes to the bar an orders the drink. "Shaken or stirred," the bartender asks to which 007 snappishly retorts, "Do I look like a give a damn?" It's the Bond-ian equivalent of the "Let the past die, kill it if you have to" mantra from *Star Wars: The Last Jedi*. You're half expecting Craig to break the fourth wall to say, "I'm not your mom and pop's Bond."

There was a moment earlier in the film that was loaded with just as much significance, though it didn't hit the audience over the head quite as much as the martini order did. When Bond was in the Bahamas, trying to keep tabs on Le Chiffre associate Alex Dimitrios, the spy tried to romance information out of Dimitrios's wife, Solange (who, at that moment, was quite pissed at her husband). Once she revealed that her husband was on his way to Miami, he had no further use for her. But that didn't mean he still didn't have time to order some room service beluga caviar and Bollinger Grand Année. Two glasses? No, just one. Not only is the world's most famous womanizer forgoing intercourse with a very beautiful and willing partner, he's not even going to have a single sip of the bubbly that's had a very visible partnership with the film franchise for nearly five decades. Unheard of!

The late Chris Cornell's *Casino Royale* theme song may have been called "You Know My Name" but it might as well have been called "You Think You Know Me, But You're Dead Wrong."

We also get to witness a mini-origin-story-within-an-origin story—in this case for the Vesper, sort of an alternative to the 007 martini. In fact, it's often mistakenly referred to as Bond's vodka martini, as if they're the same thing. And it's often called a "Vesper martini," which isn't technically accurate either.

Bond invents the drink when he changes his drink order at the casino at the last minute. During the marathon gambling session with La Chiffre, 007 summons the barman and initially asks for a dry martini. The server can barely utter "oui, monsieur" before Bond tells him, "Wait. Three measures of Gordon's (gin!), one of vodka, half a measure of Kina Lillet. Shake it over ice and then add a thin slice of lemon peel."

It was a nice little power play on Bond's part. Everyone else at the table—with the notable exception of Le Chiffre—ordered one. That included Felix Leiter (who told the waiter to "keep the fruit"), who had yet to reveal his true identity to 007.

A quick note about Kina Lillet: It often gets categorized as a vermouth, but that's inaccurate. Lillet, like vermouth, is an aromatized wine. However, unlike vermouth, it contains no wormwood. ("Vermouth" actually means "wormwood.") The Lillet recipe also includes liqueur, which is not present in vermouth. Yes, I know it sounds like a lot of hair-splitting, but don't shoot the messenger.

When Bond's fortunes reverse (after Leiter stakes him on Uncle Sam's dime so 007 can buy back into the game), 007 ultimately wins $150 million—all of Le Chiffre's clients' investment money. Le Chiffre tries to stem his losses by having his paramour, Valenka, serve Bond a poison martini. "That last hand nearly killed me," 007 quips when he returns to the gambling table after some hijinks involving a defibrillator.

He celebrates over dinner with Vesper and that's when he decides to name the drink after her. "Because of the bitter aftertaste?" she queries. "No," Bond replies. "Because once you've tasted it, that's all you'll want to drink." That is, until Vesper betrays him. (The woman, not the drink. Or maybe both.)

A couple of more quick notes on the booze-soaked adventure that is *Casino Royale*. Whenever there's a bar scene, I like to freeze-frame to check out what the bartender is stocking. (Don't try this in a movie theater.) On the back of the casino bar, I spied a lot of the usual suspects: Pernod, Jägermeister, a Bols liqueur, Luxardo, and Glenfiddich to name a few. But I was absolutely giddy when I beheld two bottles of Becherovka, side-by-side. The casino was supposed to be in Montenegro, but much of *Casino Royale* was filmed in Prague. Becherovka is, for all intents and purposes, the national spirit of the Czech Republic. It's an herbal liqueur with a history that dates back to the early nineteenth century. It's having a bit of a renaissance among bartenders in Europe and the US, so keep an eye out for this Czech-accented amaro.

Quantum of Solace

While en route to La Paz, Bolivia from somewhere in Italy, René Mathis awakens on the plane to find 007 nursing his insomnia at the first-class bar. Mathis asks Bond what he's drinking. "I don't know, what am I drinking?" 007 asks the bartender, who rattles off the ingredients to, surprise surprise, the Vesper (without naming it, of course). But the best part: When the bartender gets to Kina Lillet, he feels the need to say, "...which is not vermouth." I seriously wanted to hug the guy! Bond is already on his sixth of these by the time that this exchange takes place. The fact that the name "Vesper" is not mentioned at all in relation to this concoction speaks volumes. He's not ready to forgive his deceased love, but she's still stirring within him and he can't seem to shake her.

Skyfall

The press made a big deal out of the fact that Bond was "trading his martini for Heineken." That wasn't really true. Heineken inked a huge marketing deal with the film, so of course there had to be at least one scene where Daniel Craig's version of 007 was sipping from the iconic green bottle. It happens pretty early in the film while he's MIA, recovering on a Turkish beach after being shot and falling to his apparent death in Istanbul.

When he's bored, he decides to engage in a rather weird (and potentially deadly) drinking game in a dive bar—more like dive hut—on the beach. The object is to sip a glass of what I'm going to guess is either whisky or aged Turkish brandy without disturbing the live scorpion that sitting on one's drinking hand. Bond does quite well.

A bit later in the same bar, he helps himself to a bit of The Macallan single malt Scotch whisky, just as Wolf Blitzer comes on the TV with breaking news about a fatal explosion at MI6 headquarters in London. He seems to be holding the same bottle when he shows up in the middle of the night at M's house.

But don't worry. Bond doesn't veer too far from his cocktail comfort zone, as the franchise's next big booze partnership was with…

Spectre

…Belvedere vodka. The brand even released (in the real world) a limited-edition bottle emblazoned with the 007 logo. He could have done a lot worse. Belvedere's a fine Polish vodka made from rye, and it's a damned good base for a dirty martini (if you're into the whole vodka thing, that is). There is a bottle of it hiding behind a wall panel in L'Americain, Mr. White's favorite vacation spot in Tangier. Bond discovers it when he's holed up there with the now-deceased villain's daughter, Madeleine Swann.

Swann is possibly the one love interest who almost makes 007 confront his unhealthy habits. When he first meets her, Bond is posing as a prospective patient at her mountain clinic. (Shades of *On Her Majesty's Secret Service*?) During the intake interview,

Madeleine asks him how much alcohol he consumes. "Too much," he responds. Bond is nothing if not self-aware.

MI6-ology

Eddy Colloton and Craig Ormiston met in film school and, years later, started mixing drinks to correspond with their Bond movie viewing experiences. "We decided that if we're going to go through this much trouble, we're going to share it with everybody," Ormiston says. "And what that meant at first was to share with friends and throw themed parties and make a thing of it. It's evolved into something a little bigger than that, and now we want to share it with everyone else."

The good folks who run the boozy Bond website Licence to Drink were kind enough to share a few of the 007-inspired cocktails they developed and improved.

VESPER

Ian Fleming gets the credit for inventing this one in the 1953 novel *Casino Royale*. Bond names it after Vesper Lynd, played in the 2006 film by Eva Green (and, for those keeping score at home, by Honey Ryder herself, Ursula Andress, in the 1967 007 spoof of the same name). The original recipe called for "three measures of Gordon's gin, one of vodka, half measure of Kina Lillet," but the Licence to Drink team made a few modern modifications. Kina Lillet was reformulated in the '80s and no longer exists in its original form, so they swapped it out in favor of a Lillet Blanc-Cocchi Americano blend. Additionally, the original gin-vodka ratio would bury the Lillet-Cocchi combo, so the LTD team uses a smoother Old Tom gin with a larger measure of the aromatic blend.

- 1½ ounces Old Tom Gin (Licence to Drink recommends Hayman's)
- ¾ ounces vodka
- ½ ounce Cocchi Americano
- ¼ ounce Lillet Blanc
- Lemon twist (garnish)

Shake (of course) the first four ingredients with ice and strain into a coupe glass. Express the glass and garnish with the lemon twist.

Photo Credit: Justin Lang via Licence to Drink

SAZERAC DE FILLET OF SOUL

Inspired by the moment in *Live and Let Die* when Felix Leiter insists that Bond have a Sazerac instead of a simple glass of bourbon at the Fillet of Soul club in New Orleans, the LTD version celebrates the French and Caribbean influences on The Big Easy with the inclusion of Cognac and rum, respectively. Typically, the Sazerac recipe includes rye whiskey, but the rum replaces that.

- 1 ounce Pierre Ferrand Ambre Cognac
- 1 ounce Appleton Estate Signature Blend Rum
- ½ ounce cane sugar syrup
- 3 dashes Creole Bitters (Dashfire Classic Creole Bitters is a good option)
- 2 spritzes absinthe
- Lemon twist (for rim)

Stir the Cognac, rum, cane sugar syrup, and bitters over ice. Spritz the inside of a double rocks glass once with absinthe from an atomizer. Strain the drink into the glass and spritz again with absinthe. Generously rub a lemon peel around the glass and discard.

Photo Credit:: Jeff Cioletti

PALMYRA COLLINS

Palmyra, you'll recall, was the name of Largo's island hideaway in *Thunderball*. The Rum Collins that the Big Bad offers 007 is, of course, a riff on the classic, gin-based Tom Collins. The LTD variation lets you have your cake and eat it too, combining both spirits.

- 1½ ounces cucumber-infused white rum (see recipe below)
- ½ ounce London dry gin
- ¾ ounce Velvet Falernum
- ½ ounce lemon juice
- club soda
- Rosemary sprig (garnish)

Shake all of the ingredients except the club soda and rosemary with ice. Double strain into a highball glass filled with ice cubes. Float with the club soda and garnish with a rosemary sprig.

For the Cucumber-Infused White Rum, slice one cucumber per 750-ml bottle of white rum and infuse the cucumber in the rum for twenty-four hours.

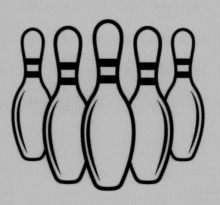

CHAPTER 10

"HEY, CAREFUL, MAN, THERE'S A BEVERAGE HERE"

Really ties the room together. Photo Credit: Jeff Cioletti

The off-screen story of *The Big Lebowski* isn't unlike that of any other movie to achieve cult status in the past four or five decades. Critics and audiences shrugged when it arrived in theaters on March 6, 1998. It did mediocre business at the domestic box office: about $17.5 million on a reported budget of $15 million.

It was the first Coen Brothers film since 1996's *Fargo*, whose pair of Oscars for Best Original Screenplay and Best Actress (Frances McDormand) understandably raised the bar for the duo's future endeavors. But the initial collective response for *Lebowski* was… well, a shrug.

I don't include myself among the indifferent. I saw the film on opening weekend with two friends and we all enjoyed it quite a bit. We didn't bother trying to compare it to *Fargo*. It's useless to compare any of the Coen films with each other. Each was a genre unto itself, and *Lebowski* was just as quotable as the rest of them. "Nobody fucks with the Jesus" is right up there with "I'll be taking these Huggies and whatever cash you got" (*Raising Arizona*) and "You know, for kids" (*The Hudsucker Proxy*). I certainly could never again listen to someone order a White Russian without hearing "Caucasian" in The Dude's signature California stoner drawl.

But for the movie-going public at large, it was almost as though the film itself was enjoying the same leisurely life that The Dude was living. It really didn't want to make any sort of effort to actually find an audience. No, *The Big Lebowski* was perfectly fine waiting for an audience to find it, just as *The Rocky Horror Picture Show* and its ilk ultimately attracted their own history-making bands of passionate misfits.

A man named Will Russell believes he knows the exact moment that *Lebowski* officially entered the rarified realm of cult classic: July 19, 2003 at the Baxter Avenue Theaters in Louisville, Kentucky. It was the second-annual "Lebowski Fest," which Russell and a friend launched on a lark the year before.

"It started as a joke," Russell recalls. "A friend of mine, Scott Shuffitt, and I were selling T-shirts at a tattoo convention for his store, The Mothership Convention. Nobody was coming to our booth. Nobody gave a shit about our shirts."

To help alleviate their boredom, they started quoting lines from *The Big Lebowski*. The folks at the neighboring booth overheard and joined in. Russell and Shuffitt suddenly realized that they were far from alone in their reverence for The Dude, et al. Hoping to connect with other like-minded abiders in the greater Louisville area, they organized a bowling party (what else?) at a rather unlikely venue: a Baptist bowling alley where both profanity and alcohol were verboten. That meant no "Shut the fuck up Donny," and no "You're not wrong, Walter. You're just an asshole." And, perhaps, most tragic of all: *no White Russians*. The hosts expected a dozen or so Achievers—the correct term for Lebowski buffs—to show up. That didn't happen. No, the number was a lot closer to 150.

Russell and Shuffitt knew they were on to something. For the 2003 edition, they moved the gathering to a more vice-friendly bowling alley. They even added a second night. This time they sold about eight hundred tickets, thanks in part to a surprise plug that Lebowski Fest got on SPIN Magazine's list of can't-miss summer events throughout America.

The screening at the Baxter Avenue Theaters—reportedly the first theatrical screening of the movie since 1998—more than sold out. To accommodate the throngs, the venue opened up a second auditorium. It didn't have a second print. It just pulled that old trick that was quite common in multiplexes when a huge summer blockbuster was playing. Projectionists would run the film from the projector in the first auditorium to the one in the second. (This doesn't happen so much these days because digital projection tends to dominate, and the studios have cracked down.) It was that evening when the Achievers became a full-fledged movement.

"When the Jesus comes on the screen for the first time—the Jesus licks his bowling ball, throws the ball, hits the strike and does the dance as the Gipsy Kings song kicks it—a guy who was dressed like the Jesus and really looked like the Jesus ran up in front of the screen and pantomimed that scene," Russell recalls. "The place just erupted—it was electric, just chills everywhere. It was the first time that that this movie, that this cult movie—which had been a commercial failure and dismissed by critics—found the fans, found us Achievers, and proud we are."

Russell was able to quit his day job and run the festival full time. It remains an annual attraction in Louisville to this day, but there are also satellite fests throughout the year in places like New York and Chicago and even across the pond in London and Edinburgh.

You can bet that wherever Achievers are congregating, the White Russians will be flowing. "It's the ceremonial beverage, so when you come to Lebowski Fest you have a White Russian," Russell declares. "The vendors love selling the shit out of the White Russian. It really ties the fest together." (I see what you did there, Will.)

An interesting side note on Russell: He's quite open about his struggles with alcoholism and mental illness. He was already sober when he started Lebowski Fest and had never tasted a White Russian until a brief, highly publicized relapse in 2015 (from which he has since recovered).

Despite the fact that he's been sober for most of the past two decades, he wouldn't think of banning The Dude's go-to cocktail. (He says alcohol is not a temptation for him. "Weed, on the other hand, is very seductive; it has a very alluring scent. Smoking weed turns me into an actual crazy person, so I don't do that.") He launched the Everything Will Be OK Project, a mental health advocacy organization.

I asked Will if he's developed a virgin White Russian to toast with during the fest, but then I realized the stupidity of that question. That's pretty much just an iced coffee with cream.

Though he himself never partakes, he's more than happy to wax philosophical about the significance of the beverage within the *Lebowski* universe and among its devout Achievers. "I think it represents The Dude," he posits. I ask him to expound on that and he says the explanation is in the ingredients. Let's deconstruct the Caucasian for a minute: vodka, cream (usually half-and-half) and coffee liqueur (usually Kahlúa, which is referenced by brand in the film a couple of times) served over ice. "It's not an energy drink," Russell points out. "It's not like a Red Bull and vodka." Sure, there's caffeine in Kahlúa, but the volume in a standard serving of the liqueur is a fraction of the stimulant found in a cup of coffee or a 12-ounce can of Coke, so it's not going to be keeping anyone up all night.

"It's a slow, creamy, kind of sweet, slow-you-down, take-it-easy-and-abide kind of beverage," Russell explains. "It really embodies the character and spirit of The Dude."

To keep things as chill, stress-free, and as Dude-like as possible, Russell typically encourages the Lebowski Fest host venues to pre-mix and batch the White Russians the night before. "The bowling alleys usually sell them for five bucks," Russell says. "Now, in the high-end theaters in New York and LA, they can be ten, fifteen bucks. In LA last year, they were selling them for twenty bucks, which made me furious."

And that, I can't abide.

ROBUST WHITE RUSSIAN

The recipe for The Dude's favorite concoction is tried and true and there's really not much you can do to jazz it up without making it cease to be a true White Russian. However, you can get a bit fancy with the ingredients if you're really trying to impress someone. And that includes the cream. Don't use some silly half-and-half from the local 7-Eleven. Your local farmer's market is likely to have a version with a bit of vegetal funk to it, thanks to the fact that the cows on small farms are usually grazing on actual grass. Usually, the stuff comes old-school, floating at the top of a glass quart or half-gallon bottle of milk. You can go completely artisanal on the coffee liqueur. For a while, Kahlúa had very little competition, but now a number of craft distillers make world-class coffee liqueurs that put the big K to shame. And now here's where it gets a bit weird. Vodka's not supposed to taste like anything. But in this case, it's going to. No, I'm not suggesting getting some artificially flavored vodka. I want to send you back to the spirit's roots. There's a brand out of Poland called Vestal that makes a series of terroir-driven craft vodkas in which you can actually taste potatoes of different vintages. Additionally, Chopin Vodka, another Polish brand, markets a line of "Single" spirits, distilled only once from either young or late harvest potato, rye, or wheat. (These are labeled as "spirits" and not vodka because they technically don't fit the definition of vodka. If you're a purist and actually want a Russian spirit in your glass, I'd suggest Polugar, a rather earthy, dirty spirit that was technically what vodka was in Russia before producers started filtering out any flavor.)

- 2 ounces Vestal Vodka, Polugar, or Chopin Single Rye
- 1 ounce craft coffee liqueur (Wigle Coffee Liqueur, House Spirits Coffee Liqueur, and St. George NOLA Coffee Liqueur are good options)
- 1 ounce fresh cream

Pour the coffee liqueur and vodka into a rocks glass over ice. Pour cream over the top and stir.

CHAPTER 11
I AM THE ONE WHO DRINKS

In the history of television, there has probably never been a better series than *Breaking Bad*. I am willing to fight you if you disagree. Those were five of the tightest seasons of television I've ever encountered, with not a single dud of an episode in any of them. No other program could inspire a spinoff or prequel series—*Better Call Saul*, of course—that not only managed to expand the *BB* universe, but to completely stand on its own and be a brilliant, serialized drama in its own right.

And, as a bonus to this drinks-loving author, it offered a treasure trove of boozy moments and Easter eggs—both real and fictional—that added an even deeper richness to the world born of creator Vince Gilligan's vision.

SCHRADERBRÄU

The most obvious (fictional) beverage to make multiple appearances throughout *Breaking Bad*'s five-season run was Drug Enforcement Agent and Walter White brother-in-law Hank Schrader's home brew.

Much has been made of Walt's Mr. Chips-to-Scarface transformation over the course of the series (Gilligan made those references himself), but that night-versus-day shift overshadowed Hank's much more underrated, gradual evolution to becoming one of the most complex, heroic and,

Did somebody knock? Photo Credit: Jeff Cioletti

dare I say, likeable characters on the show. In season one, he was pure one-dimensional machismo—the more successful, assertive alpha to Walt's milquetoast beta. Hank served merely as a conduit for Walt into the dark underbelly of crystal meth trafficking—the latter's ride-along with the former on a DEA raid connected Walt not only with that world, but reconnected the high school chemistry teacher with the former student who would become his partner in (literal) crime.

Walt's desire to provide for his family in the wake of his imminent death from lung cancer was the primary driver for his illicit actions, but Hank offered a secondary motivation. Hank was a smug representation of the sort middle-to-upper-middle class success that had eluded Walt. Of Skyler and her sister Marie, it was Marie who married "better" in the eyes of the societal establishment. Walt was better educated and possessed far more classic intelligence than Hank and, in the science teacher's mind, he deserved a piece of that pie. It was more ego than altruism that propelled Walt all along—he acknowledged as much to Skyler in "Felina," the final episode of the series. We were mostly on Walt's side. But it was in the season two episode, "Breakage," that we realized that Hank was potentially entitled to some more of our empathy.

A few episodes prior, Hank emerged the victor in a shoot-out with violently unhinged drug lord Tuco Salamanca outside the very same desert safe house that, unbeknownst to the chrome-domed DEA agent, his brother-in-law and Jesse Pinkman had just narrowly escaped (not before Jesse was able to whack Tuco in the head with a rock and pop a non-fatal dose of lead into the meth-addled kingpin's gut, leaving him to bleed out in a freshly dug grave meant for Jesse and Walt).

In "Breakage," Hank is beginning to exhibit signs of PTSD from the confrontation, and it's understandable. Despite the fact that Tuco was already injured before Hank arrived, he was far better armed than the Fed. Tuco had an automatic assault rifle. Hank had a handgun. But Hank's a crack shot and all it took was one of his bullets between Tuco's eyes to neutralize the early Breaking Baddie (see what I did there?) for good.

Still, I'd imagine that a spray of machine-gun bullets whizzing within millimeters of your own head and body would be enough to, at the very least, give you some pretty terrible recurring nightmares. So, the panic attack Hank suffered in the elevator after he just scored a promotion for his valiant Tuco takedown shouldn't have surprised anyone. Perhaps a bit more surprising was the hooky Hank played the next day to hide from this new sense of dread that the shoot-out precipitated. And, as it turns out, his favorite distraction is brewing "Schraderbräu."

He's filling bottles in his garage when we catch up with him after the elevator incident, singing the late-'70s Löwenbräu jingle ("Here's to good friends, tonight is kind of special"—those of you over forty will know the one I'm talking about), except he's replacing " Löwenbräu" with "Schraderbräu." He seems at peace, relatively, until his wife Marie opens the garage door and shatters the intimate moment between a man and his beer.

That's not all that shatters. After Marie leaves, Hank accidentally breaks a glass bottle as he's capping it, cutting his hand in the process. The bottle, of course, is Hank. And if that metaphor wasn't clear enough from that quiet moment, it reasserts itself with a literal bang toward the end of the episode. In the middle of the night, Hank awakens to what sounds like gunshots emanating from somewhere inside his house. He grabs his pistol and investigates, discovering that the noise is coming from a bunch of over-carbonated Schraderbräu blowing the caps off of several bottles. Hank might as well wear a T-shirt that reads "Warning: Contents Under Pressure."

As is the case with much of *Breaking Bad*, the episode title has multiple meanings. The literal one, as Jesse explains earlier, is the term for an expected cost of doing business. Pinkman minion (Pinkminion?) Skinny Pete gets held up by a pair of tweakers, resulting in a shortfall in expected meth-driven revenue. It's breakage, he says, like what happens at K-mart when inventory gets damaged or goes missing. Hank's hand-cutting mishap is another form of breakage. Then, of course, there's the newly "broken" Hank. Brewing, drinking, and gifting Schraderbräu to his colleagues and to local fundraisers usually brings Hank comfort. But now, he can't even find solace in his favorite hobby. It is a dark harbinger of things to come.

Naturally, beer geeks being beer geeks, we have been, for the past decade, trying to figure out exactly what style of bräu Schraderbräu is. If *Breaking Bad* took place five to ten years later, an easy answer might be "some kind of tropically fruity IPA," given the label image of Hank holding a pitcher and giving the thumbs-up while wearing a Hawaiian shirt and a lei. But those sorts of beers, while by no means nonexistent, still had a few years before they became all the rage, especially among home brewers. And, anyway, Hank's wearing a similar Hawaiian shirt (sans lei) as he bottles the stuff. My guess is that Marie took the photo of him giving two thumbs up while they were vacationing in Maui and he (or someone more graphically savvy) Photoshopped in a pitcher.

Now, about that pitcher. The vessel's contents bear a light amber, pale copper tint that leads me to believe that it's probably not a pilsner (as Löwenbräu and most beers on the market were). My guess—and you can take this with a grain of salt—is that it's an Oktoberfest style Märzen. The color is consistent and the label's font is reminiscent of that on many classic Oktoberfests, including Münchner icons like Hacker-Pschorr and Spaten. That's my answer and I'm sticking to it. No need to call my lifeline.

Turns out that I wasn't that far off. In 2019, Hank himself, actor Dean Norris, partnered with Figueroa Mountain Brewing in Buellton, California, to producer a real, live, commercial version of Schraderbrau—which was classified simply as a "German-style lager." However, he did have plans to expand the line to include—you guessed it—an Oktoberfest-style brew.

REAL-WORLD BEER & BOOZE

Breaking Bad takes place in the real world, so it's not just about fictional home brews bearing one of the main character's names. The logo for New Belgium Brewing Co.'s Fat Tire amber ale is usually visible whenever Walt walks into a bar. We even hear him order it by name in said watering holes and, if you keep your eyes peeled, you'll witness him pull a bottle or two from his fridge. It's an obvious choice. Fat Tire, brewed in Fort Collins, Colorado (and, since 2016, Asheville, North Carolina, as well), had been fairly ubiquitous throughout the western United States for some time before *Breaking Bad* premiered. And it's a no-brainer, since New Mexico borders Colorado.

On the other side of the TV screen, some lesser-known breweries wanted to get in on the act, as well, creating *Breaking Bad*-inspired beers. Since Albuquerque was pretty much a lead character in and of itself, you'd be correct to assume that local craft brewers there had quite an affinity for the series that circled their city on the map. One of the best-known Albuquerque operations at the time of the series' run, Marble Brewery, became a favorite of the cast and crew, with many frequenting the New Mexico beer maker's tasting room after long shooting days.

When the series was ending in 2013, Marble gave it a fitting sendoff with not one, but two commemorative beers celebrating the final episodes. Heisenberg Dark was a black IPA, and Walt's White Lie was a white IPA, offering a sort of yin and yang of our beloved meth cook's psyche. They weren't officially licensed, but they were produced in ultra-limited batches that didn't last much beyond the series' September 29, 2013 finale. So, it was under-the-radar enough to not make Sony Pictures Television too angry.

A company out of Auburn, California, Knee Deep Brewing Company, didn't fare quite so well. In 2018, the brewery found itself knee deep (sorry, had to) in a lawsuit with Sony over the release of Breaking Bud, a brew whose label features a riff on the TV series' own use of the periodic table for its logo—in this case, they used Br (bromine) and the fictitious Bu, instead of Br and Ba (barium) in *Breaking Bad*—as well as a cartoon character wearing the same sort of hazmat suit Walt and Jesse were known to put on from time to time. The label was a bridge too far for Sony.

Not all brands have been produced without the studio's blessing. In 2015, the producers of *Breaking Bad* partnered with (who else?) Blue Ice Vodka on a trio of limited-edition Heisenberg-themed bottles: "The One Who Knocks," "Tread Lightly," and "Say My Name." The promotion didn't last long, but it did set a rather noteworthy precedent. In the past, the US Alcohol and Tobacco Tax and Trade Bureau (TTB), has taken a hard line against any booze brand that has even the vaguest of drug references on its label. But it seems, in this case, *Breaking Bad* had a few fans working in the federal agency.

ONE MORE FOR THE ROAD

When it's last call, what do you choose? For Walter White, for whom it seemed to be the last, last call when he decides to turn himself in to the authorities in the series' penultimate episode, the parting shot would be Dimple Pinch blended Scotch whisky. Right after he calls in a tip alerting police and the Feds to his whereabouts in a New Hampshire dive bar in the final minutes of the episode titled "Granite State," he asks the bartender for a neat pour of the brand produced by the centuries-old Scottish company, Haig. Dimple Pinch is the fifteen-year-old blend in the Dimple line, named for the three dimpled ovals on each of its bottle's three vertical sides.

Walt's aborted surrender (and unfinished dram) was the first time he mentioned the spirit by name, but it's not the whiskey's first appearance in the series.

Back in the season one finale, "A No-Rough-Stuff Type Deal," Walt and Hank escape unborn baby Holly's shower to drink something "stronger than beer" (Hank's words). Sitting at the patio table, Walt pours from a bottle that is very obviously Dimple Pinch. "That's nice stuff" Hank declares, producing a cigar to pair with their tasty beverage. Hank quickly realizes his faux pas, lighting up a tobacco product in front of his lung-cancer-stricken brother-in-law. Walt is not offended in the least. In fact, he asks Hank for one of his stogies. ("You sure that's a good idea?" Hank asks. "I've already got lung cancer," Walt points out.)

This wasn't just some random moment. Cigars and Scotch whisky have long gone hand in hand, and not just with your stinky uncle. Countless articles have been devoted to the perfect cigar and whisky pairings and Scotch-and-stogie bars are a lucrative subgenre of high-end drinking establishments. Turns out the cigars are Cubans—a curious choice for a federal lawman, considering the embargo. "Sometimes the forbidden fruit tastes the sweetest," Hank notes. It prompts Walt to ponder the line society draws on what's legal and what's illegal, noting that if he and Hank were drinking whisky in 1930, they'd be breaking the law and "in another year, we'd be okay." (Well, technically, it was another *three* years, but who's counting?) It's one of the earlier rationalizations Walt uses for his chosen trade, and it's a borderline confession.

For Walt, Dimple Pinch is like the Celestial Seasonings of whisk(e)y—he uses it to celebrate the moments of his life. Aside from the impending birth of his daughter and the moment when he thinks he's reached the end of the line, he also hoists a glass after the explosive moment where he finally takes out archnemesis and fast-food-chicken magnate, Gus Fring (with more than a little help from a stroke-paralyzed Hector Salamanca). In the season five premier, "Live Free or Die" (like the later "Granite State," a reference to New Hampshire), the action picks up exactly where season four left off, with Walt declaring to Skyler, "I won." But the game isn't quite over, as ol' Heisenberg has a little more housekeeping to do. Once he disposes of every kitchen scale, measuring cup, pair of wire cutters, roll of electrical tape, and refrigeration accessory that could even remotely tie him to Fring's demise and crystal meth empire, Walt grabs a rocks glass from his cupboard and pours himself another glass of the Pinch (again, it's the bottle, folks).

However, before he even takes a single sip, he realizes there are a few more t's to cross and i's to dot.

One of those is the lily of the valley plant that played a not insignificant role in the final episodes of the prior season. Into a black trash bag it goes, flower pot and all.

Cut to a closeup of Mr. White's hand on the rocks glass with the two-finger Dimple Pinch pour. Just as the glass is about to touch his lips, he hears the front door open. Skyler, Walt Jr. (a.k.a. Flynn) and baby Holly are home. Junior's talking a mile a minute, recapping for his dad the media circus around Fring's Harvey Two-Face-enhanced demise and the discovery of the Chilean chicken mogul's hidden-in-plain-sight drug empire. Skyler's far less loquacious—downright laconic even—and that rattles Heisenberg a bit. She's clearly beginning to realize that the chemistry teacher she married is kind of a monster.

Even though Walt is still clutching the glass through all of this commotion, he never gets to finish the drink that's fifty percent celebratory, fifty percent nerve-calming—just as he leaves it un-drunk in that Granite State dive bar fourteen episodes later. In both instances, it's the ultimate expression of unfinished business.

ZAFIRO AÑEJO

We've got to talk about that tequila. You all know the one I mean. It's that ornate, blue bottle of Zafiro Añejo that Gus Fring gives to Don Eladio Vuente as a supposed peace offering in "Salud," the season four episode that changed my opinion of the Los Pollos Hermanos franchisee and made me start wishing he would survive until the end of the series. (Another spoiler alert: he didn't make it to the end of the season.)

Following an escalating conflict between Don Eladio's Juarez-based cartel and Gus Fring's operation, Gus finally agrees to head south of the border to show the Don's cooks how to produce the ultra-pure meth that's been making Fring so much money. To this end, he brings Jesse with him, as Walt has essentially taught his young business partner everything he knows and Pinkman now can achieve a Heisenberg-level of purity on his own. Also on the journey is Mike Ehrmantraut, Gus's head of security.

After the successful cooking session, Don Eladio invites the trio to his opulent estate for a pool party full of bikini-clad women. It's here where Fring gifts the narcotics kingpin with the olive-branch-in-a-bottle, Zafiro Añejo. We know this is a big deal, not only because the bottle, its agave-fronds-shaped closure, and the wooden box it's packed in are super fancy, but because Don Eladio is bordering on orgasmic to be presented with such a fine spirit. "No, imposible," he exclaims in Spanish. He also threatens his staff that he'd cut off their hands if they spill a drop.

It's hard to know exactly how añejo (aged) this añejo is. Technically, an añejo tequila is matured anywhere between one and three years. Any more than that and it's considered an extra añejo. However, extra añejo didn't exist as its own category until 2006, roughly three years before "Salud" is supposed to have taken place (the episode aired in 2011, but during the entire six-year run of *Breaking Bad*, only two years had passed on the show's timeline). It's very possible that this particular bottle of Zafiro Añejo had been filled long before 2009 and, therefore, labeled only as "añejo." When it pours, it looks like it's somewhere between completely colorless and faint gold. In that respect, it more closely resembles a blanco or, at most, a reposado. However, it's not uncommon for producers to filter out the color imparted by the barrel before bottling an añejo. Don Julio 70 Añejo Claro is a prime example of this. It's aged in oak for eighteen months before all of the oak-influenced color is stripped out.

Naturally, Don Eladio wants Gus and his crew to partake, but Fring explains that Jesse is an addict (which is true) and therefore can't drink if the Don wants any more of that super-pure crystal that Pinkman just cooked up. (And Mike's on duty and Gus is known to run a pretty tight ship, so none for Mr. Ehrmantraut either.) But there's no way Gus is going to be able to get around having a shot and he knows it. In fact, Eladio insists that Fring drink first. After all, if Gus consumes some, it couldn't possibly be poisoned, could it? Satisfied, the Don shouts a hearty, "Salud" (hence, the episode's title) and he and his goons drink the totally-not-poisoned tequila.

Of course, you know how this story ends. Gus excuses himself to go vomit in the bathroom as all others who've enjoyed a nip of Zafiro Añejo (including the Don himself) convulse and die by the pool. Fring comes pretty close to dying as well, but there's a medical team and a blood transfusion waiting nearby. "He thought of everything," an astonished Jesse, who wasn't in on the plan, proclaims in the next episode.

It should come as no shock to anyone that Zafiro is a fictitious brand. I couldn't imagine any tequila marketer signing off on the product placement deal after discovering that your spirit is going to be used in an epic, mass-poisoning scene. But I choose to think of it as a master-level double-cross that should be inducted into the con hall of fame, if there was such a thing. Since that season four moment, Zafiro Añejo seems to have become a symbol of elaborate deceptions in the *Breaking Bad* universe. The brand becomes one of the plethora of *Breaking Bad* Easter eggs that pop up from time to time on spinoff/prequel/sometimes-sequel series *Better Call Saul.* Its next appearance—or should I say "initial" appearance, since it's a prequel—occurs in the *Better Call Saul* season two opener, "Switch."

In the season one finale, the pre-Saul Jimmy McGill, Esq., learns that his beloved, electricity-averse big brother, Chuck, has been the one keeping Jimmy's legal career from advancing. This is the first of many straws that break the camel's back on Jimmy's quest to ultimately become the crooked *Breaking Bad* shyster we all know and love. Jimmy decides, for the moment at least, that he's done playing by the rules. He rejects a job offer from law firm Davis & Main and spends some lazy days by a swimming pool. Friend, colleague, and love interest Kim Wexler meets him at the local resort he's gate crashed to talk a little sense into him. Instead, she ends up joining him in a minor con against a pompous, alpha-male, stock-broker bro by the name of Ken (a Bluetooth-wearing douche who also makes an appearance on *Breaking Bad*, stealing Walt's parking space and ultimately watching his Beemer burst into flames, thanks to a bit of retributive Heisenberg-ian sabotage).

Jimmy and Kim swindle Ken into springing for some very expensive shots of Zafiro Añejo as they discuss a non-existent business opportunity. It's apparently the booze of choice for bad people about to get their comeuppance. (Ken, though, gets off with a slap on the wrist, compared with what the drink does to Don Eladio. "Ken Wins" lives to bro another day.) Like the oranges in *The Godfather* saga that often were the harbingers of death, Zafiro Añejo is a sign that someone who tries to fly too close to the sun is about to get burned.

HOIST ONE WITH HEISENBERG

WALT ROY

Dimple Pinch is mostly a sipping whisky and Walt typically drinks his neat. But it's smooth and light enough for cocktails and, as far as fifteen-year-old Scotch whiskies go, it's pretty affordable. Perhaps, the most famous Scotch-whisky-based cocktail is the Rob Roy. So, here's a slight Heisenberg-ian twist on that. I also give it a little Southwestern kick in the form of chili pepper bitters (Angostura's the typical go-to in the Rob Roy), as a nod to New Mexico.

- 2 ounces Dimple Pinch fifteen-year-old blended scotch whisky
- 1 ounce sweet vermouth
- Two dashes chili pepper bitters
- maraschino cherry

Pour whisky, vermouth, and bitters into a shaker or mixing glass filled with ice. Stir and strain into a coupe glass or rocks glass and drop in the cherry.

Photo Credit: Jeff Cioletti

THE ONE WHO KNOCKS BACK

This is a Heisenberg-enhanced boilermaker, which is not so much a cocktail as liquid pairing. In this case, it's Dimple Pinch and Walt's go-to brew, Fat Tire.

- 1 bottle (or draught pour) of New Belgium's Fat Tire Amber Ale
- 1½ ounces Dimple Pinch fifteen-year-old blended scotch whisky

Fill a pint glass with Fat Tire and a shot glass with the whisky. Sip the whisky and then the beer. Repeat until both are gone.

CHAPTER 12

SUBCULTURE AND THE SOUTH SEAS

In August 2018, I attended an event called Tiki Oasis, an annual gathering of aficionados of the faux-Polynesian aesthetic and all of its associated kitsch—and that, of course, includes rum-and-fruit-juice-centric tropical cocktails. I was attending the San Diego convention as both a tiki enthusiast and a convention speaker. Several months earlier, much to my astonishment, the Tiki Oasis team—headed up by husband-and-wife duo Otto and Baby Doe von Stroheim—accepted my proposal for a presentation titled "The Booze Renaissance Goes Tiki." I submitted it on a lark because I figured it was the only way I was going to get to attend the event. Multiday passes tend to sell out in a millisecond and the room block at the host hotel is usual full the moment registration goes live.

I'll freely admit that I had ulterior motives beyond promoting my website, The Drinkable Globe, and general South Pacific-style revelry. I was interested in exploring some of the subcultures within the subculture for this very book. Aside from Hawaiian shirts, leis, hula skirts, and drinks with tiny wood-and-paper umbrellas, pineapple garnishes, and whimsical plastic swizzle sticks, there are entire realms of allied geekery just beneath the surface of the tiki community.

You've got the musical side of things—usually rockabilly, punk, surf rock, big band, or a fusion of some or all of those. That typically overlaps with the vintage gear-head crew.

Photo Credit: Jeff Cioletti

A signature element of Tiki Oasis and its peer events throughout the country is the car show, where attendees get to peek under the hoods of hot rods from the '40s, '50s, and '60s—which also happens to be the golden age of tiki.

But the one tiki-adjacent aesthetic that I was most interested in investigating was the sort of sci-fi, creature feature, B-movie ecosystem that thrives within the retro-tropical scene.

The connection first dawned on me when I was sipping a classic Jet Pilot at Forbidden Island in Alameda, California (itself an island on the San Francisco Bay). While live bands—frequently within the genres mentioned above—are the primary entertainment in the bar, there's always some movie or TV show relevant to drinkers' interest on heavy rotation on the large flat-screen on the wall. The first time I was there, the film of choice was *Forbidden Planet* (on mute). Somehow it just worked, and not just because it has "forbidden" in its title.

At Tiki Oasis, the imagery was everywhere. For one thing, there was a late-night screening of an ultra-ultra-ultra-low-budget film called—get ready for this—*Dr. Trimrose's Cannibalistic Sex-Crazed Blood Island of the Tiki-Bots*. It's from a writer and director named Larry Lopresti and his Night Iguana Productions (whose other titles include *Blood Bath of the Bat Beast* and *The Case of the Plutonium Pin-Up Project*). It's everything you'd expect a film with that title to be, except a thousand times schlockier with more-than-generous helpings of nudity. Basically, a midnight movie on (very cheap) steroids.

During regular festival hours, there were vendors selling *Creature from the Black Lagoon* throw pillows, hand-crafted Smog Monster ceramic shot cups and Mecha Kong mugs, all sorts of retro-futuristic art objects (rockets, space travelers, you name it), and pop culture riffs on classic tiki drinking vessels. The purveyor of the latter was a company called Beeline Creative, known for its Geeki Tiki line. Characters from *Star Wars*, *Star Trek*, Marvel Comics, *Rick and Morty* (my personal favorites), and even monster breakfast cereals (Frankenberry, Count Chocula, et al.) have had their likenesses forged into mugs.

Beeline president and founder Brandon Giraldez previously worked in the toy industry, developing licensed merchandise tied to everything from *Pirates of the Caribbean* and *Smurfs* to Nintendo video game icons. "So I took kind of that toy-etic feel when we got into the drinkware business," he recalls. But tiki was not the first sandbox in which he played. The company marketed *Star Wars* character beer steins, capturing the usual rogue's gallery: Darth Vader, Boba Fett, and the like. But those were a bit on the pricier side.

"I was looking to create something that's not a fifty-dollar item, but something that could be collectible and still allow fans to buy a whole set of *Star Wars*-themed mugs and not break the bank," Giraldez says. Tiki mugs were a natural progression. Giraldez had always been a fan of tiki culture, whose renaissance was in full swing by the mid-2010s. But, Lucasfilm being Lucasfilm, the now-wholly-owned Disney subsidiary didn't sign off on the idea initially. However, Beeline decided to make some prototypes anyway and once those got in front Lucasfilm top brass, the house that George built (but ultimately flipped to the Mouse) gave it the thumbs-up.

And then Geeki Tikis like the Death Star just exploded (but in a good way). Beeline has since dedicated its efforts to the brand, rolling out—and selling out of—new characters constantly.

One of the hottest items at the 2017 Star Wars celebration in Orlando was a Jabba the Hutt and Salacious Crumb Geeki Tiki combo set. The company would allocate a certain number of those for sale at its booth each day of the convention and they were gone by the time the dealers' room floor even opened. Fans were camping out in the wee hours of the morning to get their hands on the mugs. I know because I kept being disappointed every time I went to vendor's table. (I had no interest in standing in line at three in the morning) Luckily there were still a few available to order online.

I had always seen sci-fi, comic book, and fantasy geekery as an entity that's completely separate from tiki culture. But it's really more of a Venn diagram. They've got their own, distinct circles, but there's a not insignificant area where the two intersect. You might say that space is a cantina.

"If you look at tiki—what it was with Don the Beachcomber, Trader Vic—that was a place to escape," says Giraldez. "People go to these bars to get a little bit of Polynesia, get out of the mundane world. And when you go into these places, you feel you're somewhere else. It's the same thing with the Star Wars cantina—everyone there might be fighting, but once inside, they just want to have a drink and forget about all that." (Well, tell that to Greedo.) It just so happens that Beeline expanded its Geeki Tiki line with an entire series of cantina creatures.

But Giraldez insists that his target market is not the hardcore tiki-philes (of which, he, himself, proudly admits to being one), but those relatively new to the genre or the casual enthusiasts. "The people who are the true tiki fans are in a very small bubble," he insists. "They're into anything from the time period when tiki started. The '30s, '40s and '50s were its heyday, so things like *Creature from the Black Lagoon* and B movies are all a part of that."

Some from the more devout side of tiki culture have been quite receptive to the notion of Geeki Tikis. "But within that bubble," Giraldez reveals, "we do get, 'oh, that's not tiki.' I can have the discussion about what is and what isn't tiki—but that really isn't our customer."

If there's one element that drives both camps—the Comic-Con and tiki sets—that occupies the largest intersecting space of that aforementioned Venn diagram, it's nostalgia. One of the biggest issues with some of the trendier, recently opened, craft-cocktail-centric iterations of the classic tiki bar is that they spend so much time trying to elevate and modernize the drinks. Believe me, nothing's broken, so why are they fixing it? They throw the baby out with the bath water. They sacrifice the kitschy, dark, escape-from-the-urban aesthetic, in favor of a more sterile, brightly lit, let's-paint-a-few-tropical-flowers-and-palm-fronds-on-the-wall vibe, completely neglecting everything that makes tiki great. Tiki fanatics don't necessarily long for a tropical getaway—they want to escape to the South Pacific of a time when the popular movie was…well, *South Pacific*.

In fact, the theme for Tiki Oasis 2018 was South Seas Cinema, and there were more than a handful of attending revelers dressed like characters from *South Pacific* and other sand, surf, and coconut entertainment of the era.

I also counted at least forty women with Betty Page hairdos and at least three times that number donning vintage, late-'50s-style bikinis and long, flowing caftans. (There was even an organized meet-up of the caftan crew, who strutted their stuff like a parade throughout the grounds of Crowne Plaza San Diego. I overheard one saying that she and her compatriots should've worn Mrs. Roper wigs to really sell the look.)

Their male counterparts were equally game. Dozens of men in fedoras—the vintage kind, not the ironic hipster type—as well as porkpie hats and sailor caps. There was at least one guy who went full Gilligan! A couple of dudes (I'm assuming they're dudes, but what do I know?) had aloha shirts and shorts over full-body chimpanzee outfits. I tip my hat to them because it was uncharacteristically hot and humid for San Diego. Usually you can expect it to be around 75 to 78 degrees Fahrenheit, even in August. But the high that day was hovering around 90. Wearing an ape costume takes real dedication, even in the mildest of temperatures.

Five minutes of such visual stimuli was all it took for me to have my (not-so-astute) eureka moment: This is cosplay in its purest form. Three weeks earlier, the city was overrun with Klingons, Stormtroopers, Walter Whites, Wolverines, Wonder Women, Harley Quinns, and Black Widows. There was as much passion and attention to detail in the Tiki Oasis attire as there was at Comic-Con. When you look at the phenomenon from that vantage point, both subcultures are more alike than they are different. And it was no accident that, on the day when I presented my drinking symposium at the tropical event, I was wearing a tiki shirt populated by Star Wars cantina creatures, designed by renowned Southern California artist Shag (real name: Josh Agle). I was standing at the nexus of the two worlds, and I was loving every second of it.

But my greatest discovery had little to do with where these worlds intersect. The whole time I had been searching for geek culture within the tiki realm. And I found plenty of it. But what I had naively misunderstood all along was that tiki was its own form of geekery—independent of whatever sub-nerdery it invited. Before I had a foot in tiki. Now I'm all in.

1: Frankie's Tiki Rom in Las Vegas, NV, 2: Tiki Oasis in San Diego, CA, 3: Forbidden Island; Alameda, CA, 4: Lost Lake in Chicago, IL. Photo Credit: Jeff Cioletti

BLACK LAGOON

In keeping with the Golden Age of B movies aesthetic that goes hand in hand with the tiki world, here's a recipe designed for Geeki Tiki's Gill-man mug, inspired by the monster movie classic, *The Creature from the Black Lagoon.* Of course, you can enjoy it any tiki- or tiki-adjacent vessel if you can't get your hands on ol' Mr. Gill. This one's the brainchild of Nashville bartender and consultant Jonathan B. Howard.

- 1 ounce Clément Blanc Agricole Rhum
- 1 ounce Bacardi Carta Blanca Rum
- ¾ ounce Midori
- ¾ ounce fresh lemon juice
- ¼ ounce Green Chartreuse
- ¼ ounce salt solution (1 part salt to 1.5 parts water)
- Dash of activated charcoal

Add all ingredients to a mixing tin with crushed ice. Shake vigorously and strain into a Gill-man mug (or similarly horrifying vessel). Garnish with underwater vegetation (kelp, nori—whatever you can get your hands on).

The Black Lagoon cocktail in Geeki Tikis Gill-Man mug.
Photo Credit: Angelina Melody Photography (special thanks to Beeline Creative)

EPILOGUE

Epiphanies seldom occur in real life. Movies, plays, TV shows, and books make them seem like everyday occurrences because they're overused to the point of cliché. Therefore, it is with a heavy heart, that I inform you I am about to become that cliché.

I'm at one of the many work tables in the café-nightclub hybrid that is the lobby of the Citizen M London Bankside hotel, typing away on my Macbook Pro, racing to meet the publisher's deadline for the book you're reading right now. It's my favorite hotel in my favorite city—a city I've visited more than fifteen times since my initial trip in March of 1994 when I was on spring break in my senior year of college. That was my first journey overseas and I fell in love with London instantly. For the past quarter century, even as my travels have brought me to hundreds of cities in dozens of countries on six continents, London has remained my happy place. My affection for the United Kingdom and its capital city may have been a constant through all of those years, the elements that continue to attract me to London have evolved.

Initially, *Doctor Who* had quite a bit to do with it. This is, after all, the city where it all began, back on November 23, 1963. My friend Mathias, a.k.a. Matt, and I first discovered the long-running British series on our local PBS station, New Jersey Network, in early 1984. At the age of twelve, I had neither the means nor the permission to travel across the Atlantic, so I was forced to love England from afar for the next decade. For a kid who would not fly on a plane until he was eighteen, London was a bucket list destination—long before the term "bucket list" would even enter the vernacular. I romanticized and idealized the destination long before I visited it, thanks to a time-traveler who hailed from a planet billions of light-years away from Great Britain.

When I finally did get to go, *Doctor Who* had been off the air for about five years. It seemed, much to my disappointment, as though Londoners had all but forgotten the program that ran on the BBC for twenty-six years. I was able to find some evidence of its existence at the city's Museum of the Moving Image which, at the time, housed life-sized Dalek and K-9 models in a small sci-fi ghetto that also included Star Wars Stormtrooper armor.

At the time, I drowned my sorrows in a recent UK-based discovery of mine, the fermented beverage that would carry me through most of the next decade of my life: hard cider. My experience with beer at the time was the experience of just about every '90s university student: Beer was cheap and disgusting. I would buy $8.99 twenty-four-pack cases of Busch Light for parties because I wasn't looking for flavor, I was just looking to get hammered as quickly as possible.

A few months before I boarded my first Virgin Atlantic flight from Newark to Heathrow, a friend introduced me to Woodpecker Cider at a New Brunswick, New Jersey bar called the Ale 'N 'Wich—which, as you probably can guess from its name, fancied itself an English-style pub (though, as I would soon learn, it wasn't doing a very good job replicating that experience). At that moment, it was exactly the sort of thing I was looking for. I didn't really like beer (because I was still a few years away from actually tasting good beer), nor did I like the taste of just about anything alcoholic that I was consuming at the time. Most of the time I was just mixing a bunch of incongruous ingredients to mask the flavor of whatever hard liquor I could get my hands on. There were also the shots of Southern Comfort that I tried to wolf down as quickly as possible. I still wince at the sense-memory of that stuff. But cider—or what passed for cider in the '90s—actually tasted good to me. I had a much higher tolerance for sweet things in those days, which was a good thing, considering that virtually all of the stuff one could find stateside twenty-odd years ago was of the diabetes-inducing variety.

In London, however, I tried as many brands as the pubs would carry and discovered that there were many on the drier side that offered a nice counterpoint to the more sugar-forward selections (though still off-puttingly sweet by today's standards, as well as the standards of my own palate two decades later). More importantly, the experience gave me an entirely new reason to love the United Kingdom: an entire category of drinks that barely existed on my side of the Atlantic. The moment I stepped back on US soil, I began obsessing about my next (hypothetical) trip there. I even went so far as to call the British Consulate to inquire about work visas.

I'd have to wait another two years, but I did make it back and was happy to find that all of the cider was right where I had left it.

Cider remained my go-to beverage for another seven years or so. When it wasn't available (which was often the case in American bars), my fallback was a gin and tonic. I had yet to even learn the difference between vodka and gin—or the fact that the latter was, itself, a distinctly British spirit. In January 2003, I started working at *Beverage World* magazine, which opened my eyes to the drink that would define the next decade or so of my life: craft beer. The American brewing revolution that was on the cusp of its second wave of explosive growth introduced me to a wealth of classic styles that were never on my radar. Their US iterations made me keen to explore those styles' European origins.

Initially it was Belgium. For the first few years of my burgeoning beer geekery, I drank little else than Belgian and Belgian-style beer. There were a few Belgian bars in New York at the time (my favorites were Petite Abeille and Vol de Nuit), which became my regular haunts. I made my first pilgrimage (of many) to Belgium in late 2005.

I realized I was cocooning myself a bit too tightly in big, bold Belgian beers and I allowed myself to branch out a bit. Once I realized it wasn't all about mega-ABVs, and that a brew with 4 percent alcohol by volume could be just as delightful (if not more so), I was ready to embrace traditional English cask ales. And, to paraphrase the sixth Doctor, it seemed not a moment too soon.

In early 2008, I tagged along on my wife's London business trip—it would be my first time there in more than five years and our second visit as a couple. Even more significantly, it was my first UK trip as a beer lover, especially one with a new appreciation for the English brewing tradition. I was itching to put the Campaign for Real Ale's (CAMRA) book of London pub crawls to good use. But there was an added bonus on this particular visit: It was the first time I'd be in the United Kingdom since *Doctor Who*'s triumphant relaunch as a regular BBC series. Indeed, it was the first time I was there when the show was on the air at all.

I really didn't know what to expect. By then, it was fairly popular in the US, far more than it was back in the classic series' PBS days, but it would be a good year or so before it truly became part of the American cult-TV zeitgeist.

I was in for a very pleasant surprise. The Doctor was *in*. Billboards on Charing Cross Road. Toys and memorabilia dominating store shelves. David Tennant on Jools Holland's *Hootenanny*—not to mention the welcome video on the Heathrow Express train! This London was the antithesis of the Whovian wasteland it was in the '90s. It was everything I wished it had been back in those days and a thousand times more. (Yes, I'm aware that the production team actually shoots most of the series in Cardiff, Wales.) I could scarcely avoid it between pints and pubs as I chronicled my cask ale crawl. It didn't dawn on me until a decade later—here, in the lobby of the Citizen M London Bankside—that the January 2008 London trip was the week that my passions inextricably aligned: beverage geekery and cult entertainment geekery, tied up with a beautiful ribbon called London. It was that dreaded, overused e-word: epiphany.

The revelation forced me to ponder how so many other roads lead back here. *Star Wars*, for all intents and purposes, started here. It is, after all, the home base of Elstree Studios, the filming location for most of *A New Hope*. And, as I write this, not incredibly far from where I am sitting, J.J. Abrams is about two months into filming *Episode IX* at Pinewood Studios—not coincidentally the production home for our favorite British secret agent. They actually renamed part of Pinewood as the Albert R. Broccoli 007 stage, honoring the franchise's late producer. A significant number of the Bond films also included location shoots on the streets of London.

Heck, even all-American comic book icons have English roots. The four Christopher Reeve Superman films were shot at Pinewood, Elstree, and Shepperton Studios. And remember

Tim Burton's surreal, German Expressionism-inspired vision of Gotham City in his first Batman film? That was Pinewood. Let's not forget, two of the writers who essentially invented science fiction—Mary Wollstonecraft Shelley and H.G. Wells, of course—spent at least part of their lives in the English capital.

With that sort of pedigree, how could you not believe that there's some sort of psychic energy that envelops London and its surrounding environs? It must be what constantly draws me here. It's unnatural for me not to get tired of making return trips to the same place over and over again. But every time I board a Heathrow-bound flight, I experience a giddiness I seldom feel for other destinations, especially those I've visited more than once. And when I leave, I immediately begin figuring out an excuse to return as soon as possible. The plane wheels barely touch the ground on US soil before I book the next dates at the Citizen M London Bankside.

Beyond the mystical, magnetic force drawing me back—I don't truly believe in that, it just makes for a nice conceit when I'm wrapping up a book—it's really London's flexibility and willingness to accommodate my changing tastes that attracts me the most. It's not even that my tastes are changing per se, I just keep adding new interests on top of the old ones, subtracting little or nothing from those earlier pursuits.

Case in point: 2013. November 23 of that year was the fiftieth anniversary of the broadcast of the very first episode of *Doctor Who*. I was determined to be in London on that exact day, a little more than seven months after my last visit. When the BBC announced that there would be the *Doctor Who* convention to end all *Doctor Who* conventions on the 23rd (and the rest of the weekend), that sealed the deal for me. The icing on the fiftieth birthday cake was that the BBC was producing a special anniversary episode—ultimately titled, appropriately enough, "The Day of the Doctor"—which I was going to get to watch in London. The icing on that icing was that the network was simulcasting it in cinemas across the globe and I got to enjoy it in the city where it all started, exactly fifty years ago, almost to the minute. I even convinced Mathias/Matt, who was then living in Geneva, Switzerland, to fly in for the night so we could keep a promise we made to our twelve-year-old selves.

That was right around the time that my interest in spirits equaled and maybe even started to surpass my affinity for beer. I found myself ordering whisk(e)y on more occasions than I was ordering beer. And London had plenty of that for me, mostly by way of England's neighbor to the north. It was also the height of the Great Gin Renaissance (caps mine), a rediscovery and reinvention of the botanical spirit for which the city was most famous. London dry gin is an official style, after all, and the one most people around the world think of when they think of "gin." It was an opportunity for me to get reacquainted with the spirit, especially since my past experience was mostly watered down G&Ts with gin that tasted like lighter fluid and a sparkling beverage that barely qualified as tonic.

Just as gin reconquered Europe in the 2010s, it found a new loyal subject in this avid imbiber who was ready to take the advice of the first book he wrote and step out of his drinking comfort zone. Suddenly gin became my reason (read: excuse) to fly to London at least once a year. In February 2016, 2017, and 2018, when the British immigration officers asked me the purpose of my visit, my answer on each occasion was "Gin Festival." The officers always voiced their approval, just as they had when I told them I was coming to town to drink real ale in their pubs. "You seem like a man of discerning taste," I recall one of them saying. (Why do American immigration officers have to be so stiff? Homeland Security should send new recruits to the UK for social skills training).

Those very same pubs in which I indulged in many a pint on that initial 2008 cask ale crawl now were touting their quite extensive gin lists in addition to their impressive beer selections. "Home is Where the Gin Is" and "It's Gin O'Clock" were just a couple of the signs I saw posted in these ale-centric locals. I was still doing my usual run to The Who Shop, the East London emporium of all things Time Lord, but juniper and quinine were fueling my journey more than hops and malt were. Suddenly, new distilleries were springing up throughout the city as quickly as new breweries.

It's as though the modern history of London drinking was the modern history of what I was drinking. I wonder what form that will take five, ten years from now. Why will I be traveling here? What will be on my TV screen (well, my laptop screen)? And what will be in my glass? I have no idea. But I do know it's always going to be one a hell of a ride.

Allons-y!

ACKNOWLEDGMENTS

In a sense, this book has been a lifetime in the making, compiling elements that have been taking up space in my brain since I was old enough to turn on a TV and sit up straight in a movie theater. That means I've got more than four decades worth of people to thank.

First, I'd like to thank my agent, Max Sinsheimer, who constantly lit a fire under my ass to whip the *Drink Like a Geek* book proposal into shape. It's a much better book because of him. And, of course, I have to thank Chris McKenney, Brenda Knight, Robin Miller, Elina Diaz (who designed this thing!) and everyone at Mango Publishing for agreeing to take a chance on this nerdy idea (and for their saint-like patience).

Big shout-outs to my cousin Tom (TJ) Cioletti for the sushi-and-sake-fueled discussion on comic books in Studio City and to Andrew Kaplan for the Trek talk over wings and cocktails in Forest Hills. Also, cheers to Laura De Young and Robin Maddock for helping me navigate the modern videogame world. Laura's geekiness runs deep, as we used to talk Star Wars during our high school days in northern New Jersey. I also raise a glass to Brandon Giraldez, Eddy Colloton, Craig Ormiston, Brett Ferencz, Ben Peal, and Will Russell for all of their cross-genre insights. (Double thanks to Eddy and Craig for their cocktail contributions.)

Massive toast to Ben Paré for always coming through with the most innovative drinks recipes. Glad we could collaborate again on this book. And a huge clinking-of-the-glass to Airto Cramer and the Tales & Spirits team in Amsterdam for offering up the

Star Wars recipes, as well as Joseph Quintero at Café 44 in Alexandria for "Butterbeer's Older Brother."

I'm privileged to get to write about booze for a living and it's all because so many publications and websites are bonkers enough to work with me: Kate Bernot (who, as of this writing, had the most listened-to episode on my podcast, The Drinkable Globe), Kevin Pang and Gwen Ihnat at The Takeout, William Tish at Beverage Media, Erica Duecy and Jen Laskey at SevenFifty Daily, Margie A.S. Lerhman at the American Craft Spirits Association, Brian Christensen at Artisan Spirit, Stefanie Gans at Northern Virginia Magazine, Jessica Jacobsen at Beverage Industry, and Jeff Klineman and Ray Latif at BevNet. And then of course, there's all around great guy and writing sage John Holl, whose advice and harassment have been invaluable.

I've shared a drink or three with so many people throughout my life and career and I'd like to buy another round for all of them (figuratively—I'm not made of money), in no particular order: Joe and Colleen Orlando, Jenn and Geoff Clark, Karen Auerbach, Roland Ottewell, Joanna and Jeff Bauman, Jim and Lisa Flynn, Sarah and Giancarlo Annese, Renee Hickerson, Dean Bardouka, Laura Schacht, Don and Michele Tse, John Kleinchester, Natasha Bahrs, Leila Hamdan, Mark Gillespie, Maureen Ogle, Erika Rietz, April Darcy, Emily Wax, Marty and Temple Moore, Danielle Eddy, Rachel Bonnewell, Mary Kate and Ben Mack, Augie Carton, Justin Kennedy, Brian Yaeger, Ken Weaver, Bryan Roth, Adam Fulrath, Mike and Kristina Mansbridge, Wouter Bosch, Erika Bolden, Brandon Buck, Schuyler Deming, Farshad Aduli, Preston and Allen O'Neil, Carrie Havranek, Paul Hletko, Mark Shilling, Steve Johnson, Lew Bryson, Em Sauter, Kara Newman, Camper English, Darek Bell, Davin de Kergommeaux, Dan Dunn, Emily Pennington,

Alexandra Clough, Jason Horn, Alena Kerins, Will Salas, Erik Roth, Jen Kirby, Heather Landi, Rosanna Bulian, Andrea Foote, Lisa Adams, Erin Fiden, Alex Luboff, Jordan Wicker, Tyler Lloyd, Amber Gallaty, Stephen Lyman, Christopher Pelligrini, Noriyuki Yamashita, Jamie Graves, Rhonda Kallman, Jeff Alworth, Amanda Cioletti, Rob McCaughey, Randy Mosher, Julia Herz and far too many other people to name.

I can't forget Mathias Bolton, even though the militant teetotaler that he is will never forgive me for including him in a book about booze. Don't worry, Matt, you're in it for the *Doctor Who*, not the alcohol.

Big hug to mom and dad for bringing me into this world and for never taking me out of it, even though I've given you plenty of reasons over the years to do so.

And to my wife Craige, who I once dragged across the country to a *Doctor Who* convention when we only just started dated and she had zero interest in such geekery.

I also would like to dedicate this book to the memory of Jenny Roth. You'll always be in our thoughts, Jenny.

Photo Credit: Craige Moore ————

RESOURCES

BOOKS

Adams, Douglas. *The Restaurant at the End of the Universe.* London, UK: Pan Books, 1980.

Martin, George R.R. *A Game of Thrones (A Song of Ice and Fire Book 1).* New York: Bantam Books, 1996.

Martin, George R.R. *A Clash of Kings (A Song of Ice and Fire Book 2).* New York: Bantam Books, 1999.

Martin, George R.R. *A Storm of Swords (A Song of Ice and Fire Book 3).* New York: Bantam Books, 2000.

Martin, George R.R. *A Feast for Crows (A Song of Ice and Fire Book 4).* New York: Bantam Books, 2005.

Martin, George R.R. *A Dance with Dragons (A Song of Ice and Fire Book 5).* New York: Bantam Books, 2011.

Rowling, J.K. *Harry Potter and the Philosopher's Stone.* New York: Scholastic, 1997.

Rowling, J.K. *Harry Potter and the Chamber of Secrets.* New York: Scholastic, 1999.

Rowling, J.K. *Harry Potter and the Prisoner of Azkaban.* New York: Scholastic, 1999.

Rowling, J.K. *Harry Potter and the Goblet of Fire.* New York: Scholastic, 2000.

Rowling, J.K. *Harry Potter and the Order of the Phoenix.* New York: Scholastic, 2003.

Rowling, J.K. *Harry Potter and the Half-Blood Prince.* New York: Scholastic, 2005.

Rowling, J.K. *Harry Potter and the Deathly Hallows.* New York: Scholastic, 2007.

COMIC BOOKS AND GRAPHIC NOVELS

Bendis, Brian Michael and Michael Gaydos. *Jessica Jones: Alias Vol. 1 (Collecting Alias* issues 1–9). New York: Marvel, 2015 (originally published in comic book form 2001–2002).

Michelnie, David, Bob Layton, John Romita Jr., and Carmine Infantino. *Iron Man: Demon in a Bottle (Collecting Iron Man* issues 120–128). New York: Marvel, 2006 (originally published in comic book form, 1979).

Mignola, Mike. *Hellboy Vol. 2: Wake the Devil (Collecting Hellboy: Wake the Devil* issue 1–5). Milwaukie, Oregon: Dark Horse Books, 1997.

Mignola, Mike. *Hellboy #3: The Island Part 1*. Milwaukie, Oregon: Dark Horse Comics, 2005.

Mignola, Mike. *Hellboy #4: The Island Part 2*. Milwaukie, Oregon: Dar Horse Comics, 2005.

MOVIES

James Bond

Dr. No. Directed by Terence Young. 1962. London, UK & Beverly Hills, California; Eon Productions & United Artists, XFinity On-Demand, 2018.

From Russia with Love. Directed by Terence Young, 1963; London, UK & Beverly Hills, California; Eon Productions & United Artists, XFinity On-Demand, 2018.

Goldfinger. Directed by Guy Hamilton. 1964. London, UK & Beverly Hills, California: Eon Productions & United Artists, XFinity On-Demand, 2018.

Thunderball. Directed by Terence Young. 1965. London, UK & Beverly Hills, California: Eon Productions & United Artists, XFinity On-Demand, 2018.

You Only Live Twice. Directed by Lewis Gilbert. 1967. London, UK & Beverly Hills, California: Eon Productions & United Artists, XFinity On-Demand, 2018.

On Her Majesty's Secret Service. Directed by Peter R. Hunt. 1969. London, UK & Beverly Hills, California: Eon Productions & United Artists, XFinity On-Demand, 2018.

Diamonds Are Forever. Directed by Guy Hamilton. 1971. London, UK & Beverly Hills, California: Eon Productions & United Artists, XFinity On-Demand, 2018.

Live and Let Die. Directed by Guy Hamilton. 1973. London, UK & Beverly Hills, California: Eon Productions & United Artists, XFinity On-Demand, 2018.

The Man with the Golden Gun. Directed by Guy Hamilton. 1974. London, UK & Beverly Hills, California: Eon Productions & United Artists. XFinity On-Demand, 2018.

The Spy Who Loved Me. Directed by Lewis Gilbert. 1977. London, UK & Beverly Hills, California: Eon Productions & United Artists. XFinity On-Demand, 2018.

Moonraker. Directed by Lewis Gilbert. 1979. London, UK & Beverly Hills, California: Eon Productions & United Artists. XFinity On-Demand, 2018.

For Your Eyes Only. Directed by John Glen. 1981. London, UK & Beverly Hills, California: Eon Productions & United Artists. XFinity On-Demand, 2018.

Octopussy. Directed by John Glen. 1983. London, UK & Beverly Hills, California: Eon Productions & MGM/United Artists. XFinity On-Demand, 2018.

A View to a Kill. Directed by John Glen. 1985. London, UK & Beverly Hills, California: Eon Productions & MGM/United Artists. XFinity On-Demand, 2018.

The Living Daylights. Directed by John Glen. 1987. London, UK & Beverly Hills, California: Eon Productions & MGM/United Artists. XFinity On-Demand, 2018.

Licence to Kill. Directed by John Glen. 1989. London, UK & Beverly Hills, California: Eon Productions & MGM/United Artists. MGM Home Video (DVD).

GoldenEye. Directed by Martin Campbell. 1995. London, UK & Beverly Hills, California: Eon Productions & MGM/United Artists. XFinity On-Demand, 2018.

Tomorrow Never Dies. Directed by Roger Spottiswoode. 1997. London, UK & Beverly Hills, California: Eon Productions & MGM/United Artists. MGM Home Video (DVD).

The World Is Not Enough. Directed by Michael Apted. 1999. London, UK & Beverly Hills, California: Eon Productions & MGM/United Artists. MGM Home Video (DVD).

Die Another Day. Directed by Lee Tamahori. 2002. London, UK & Beverly Hills, California. Eon Productions & MGM/United Artists. MGM Home Video (DVD).

Casino Royale. Directed by Martin Campbell. 2006. London, UK & Beverly Hills, California. Eon Productions & MGM/United Artists. XFinity On-Demand, 2018.

Quantum of Solace. Directed by Marc Forster. 2008. London, UK & Beverly Hills, California. Eon Productions & MGM/United Artists. XFinity On-Demand, 2018.

Skyfall. Directed by Sam Mendes. 2012. London, UK & Beverly Hills, California. Eon Productions & MGM/United Artists. MGM Home Video (DVD).

Spectre. Directed by Sam Mendes. 2015. London, UK & Beverly Hills, California. Eon Productions & MGM/United Artists. MGM Home Video (DVD).

Star Wars

Star Wars Episode IV: A New Hope. Directed by George Lucas. 1977. Los Angeles, California. Twentieth Century Fox.

Star Wars Episode V: The Empire Strikes Back. Directed by Irvin Kirschner. 1980. Los Angeles, California. Twentieth Century Fox.

Star Wars Episode VI: Return of the Jedi. Directed by Richard Marquand. 1983. Los Angeles, California. Twentieth Century Fox.

Star Wars Episode I: The Phantom Menace. Directed by George Lucas. 1999. Los Angeles, California. Twentieth Century Fox.

Star Wars Episode II: Attack of the Clones. Directed by George Lucas. 2002. Los Angeles, California. Twentieth Century Fox.

Star Wars Episode III: Revenge of the Sith. Directed by George Lucas. 2005. Los Angeles, California. Twentieth Century Fox.

Star Wars Episode VII: The Force Awakens. Directed by J.J. Abrams. 2015. Burbank, California. Walt Disney Studios.

Rogue One: A Star Wars Story. Directed by Gareth Edwards. 2016. Burbank, California. Walt Disney Studios.

Star Wars Episode VIII: The Last Jedi. Directed by Rian Johnson. 2017. Burbank, California. Walt Disney Studios.

Solo: A Star Wars Story. Directed by Ron Howard. 2018. Burbank, California. Walt Disney Studios.

Star Trek

Star Trek: The Motion Picture. Directed by Robert Wise. 1979. Hollywood, California. Paramount Pictures.

Star Trek II: The Wrath of Khan. Directed by Nicholas Meyer. 1982. Hollywood, California. Paramount Pictures.

Star Trek III: The Search for Spock. Directed by Leonard Nimoy. 1984. Hollywood, California. Paramount Pictures.

Star Trek IV: The Voyage Home. Directed by Leonard Nimoy. 1986. Hollywood, California. Paramount Pictures.

Star Trek V: The Final Frontier. Directed by William Shatner. 1989. Hollywood, California. Paramount Pictures.

Star Trek VI: The Undiscovered Country. Directed by Nicholas Meyer. 1991. Hollywood, California. Paramount Pictures.

Star Trek: Generations. Directed by David Carson. 1994. Hollywood, California. Paramount Pictures.

Star Trek: First Contact. Directed by Jonathan Frakes. 1996. Hollywood, California. Paramount Pictures.

Star Trek: Insurrection. Directed by Jonathan Frakes. 1998. Hollywood, California. Paramount Pictures.

Star Trek: Nemesis. Directed by Stuart Baird. 2002. Hollywood, California. Paramount Pictures.

Star Trek. Directed by J.J. Abrams. 2009. Hollywood, California. Paramount Pictures.

Star Trek: Into Darkness. Directed by J.J. Abrams. 2013. Hollywood, California. Paramount Pictures.

Star Trek: Beyond. Directed by Justin Lin. 2016. Hollywood, California. Paramount Pictures.

Harry Potter

Harry Potter and the Sorcerer's Stone. Directed by Chris Columbus. 2001. Burbank, California. Warner Bros.

Harry Potter and the Chamber of Secrets. Directed by Chris Columbus. 2002. Burbank, California. Warner Bros.

Harry Potter and the Prisoner of Azkaban. Directed by Alfonso Cuarón. 2004. Burbank, California. Warner Bros.

Harry Potter and the Goblet of Fire. Directed by Mike Newell. 2005. Burbank, California. Warner Bros.

Harry Potter and the Order of the Phoenix. Directed by David Yates. 2007. Burbank, California. Warner Bros.

Harry Potter and the Half-Blood Prince. Directed by David Yates. 2009. Burbank, California. Warner Bros.

Harry Potter and the Deathly Hallows Part 1. Directed by David Yates. 2010. Burbank, California. Warner Bros.

Harry Potter and the Deathly Hallows Part 2. Directed by David Yates. 2011. Burbank, California. Warner Bros.

Other Movies

The Big Lebowski. Directed by Joel Coen & Ethan Coen. 1998. Universal City, California. Polygram Filmed Entertainment & Universal Pictures.

Hellboy. Directed by Guillermo del Toro. 2004. Culver City, California. Columbia Pictures.

Hellboy II: The Golden Army. Directed by Guillermo del Toro. 2008. Universal City, California. Universal Pictures.

TELEVISION

Doctor Who

Doctor Who, Season 2 (classic series), episode 37, "The Time Meddler Part 1: The Watcher." Directed by Douglas Camfield. Written by Dennis Spooner. Aired 3 July 1965 on BBC, accessed 2018 on BritBox streaming.

Doctor Who, Season 2 (classic series), episode 38, "The Time Meddler Part 2: The Meddling Monk." Directed by Douglas Camfield. Written by Dennis Spooner. Aired 10 July 1965 on BBC, accessed 2018 on BritBox streaming.

Doctor Who, Season 2 (classic series), episode 39, "The Time Meddler Part 3: A Battle of Wits." Directed by Douglas Camfield. Written by Dennis Spooner. Aired 17 July 1965 on BBC, accessed 2018 on BritBox streaming.

Doctor Who, Season 2 (classic series), episode 40, "The Time Meddler Part 4: Checkmate." Directed by Douglas Camfield. Written by Dennis Spooner. Aired 24 July 1965 on BBC, accessed 2018 on BritBox streaming

Doctor Who, Season 3 (classic series), episode 34, "The Gunfighters Part 1: A Holiday for the Doctor." Directed by Rex Tucker. Written by Donald Cotton. Aired 30 April 1966 on BBC, accessed 2018 on BritBox streaming.

Doctor Who, Season 3 (classic series), episode 35, "The Gunfighters Part 2: Don't Shoot the Pianist." Directed by Rex Tucker. Written by Donald Cotton. Aired 7 May 1966 on BBC, accessed 2018 on BritBox streaming.

Doctor Who, Season 3 (classic series), episode 36, "The Gunfighters Part 3: Johnny Ringo." Directed by Rex Tucker. Written by Donald Cotton. Aired 14 May 1966 on BBC, accessed 2018 on BritBox streaming.

Doctor Who, Season 3 (classic series), episode 37, "The Gunfighters Part 4: The OK Corral." Directed by Rex Turcker. Written by Donald Cotton. Aired 21 May 1966.

Doctor Who, Season 4 (classic series), episode 1: "The Smugglers Part 1." Directed by Julia Smith. Written by Brian Hayles. Aired 10 September 1966 on BBC, animated reconstruction by Who Recons accessed on YouTube 2018.

Doctor Who, Season 4 (classic series), episode 2: "The Smugglers Part 2." Directed by Julia Smith. Written by Brian Hayles. Aired 17 September 1966 on BBC, animated reconstruction by Who Recons accessed on YouTube 2018.

Doctor Who, Season 9 (classic series), episode 1, "The Day of the Daleks Episode 1," Aired 1 January 1972 on BBC, accessed 2018 on BritBox streaming.

Doctor Who. Season 10 (classic series), episodes 1–4, "The Three Doctors." Directed by Lennie Mayne. Written by Bob Baker & Dave Martin. Aired 30 Dec 1972 to 20 Jan 1973 on BBC; June 1985 on New Jersey Network, accessed 2018 on iTunes.

Doctor Who, Season 20 (classic series), episode 23, "The Five Doctors." Directed by Peter Moffat, John Nathan-Turner, and Pennant Roberts. Written by Terence Dicks, Aired 23 November, 1983 on BBC and New Jersey Network.

Doctor Who, Season 1 (revived series), episode 4, "Aliens of London." Directed by Keith Boak. Written by Russell T. Davies. Aired 16 April 2005 on BBC, accessed 2018 on iTunes.

Doctor Who, Season 1 (revived series), episode 5, "World War Three." Directed by Keith Boak. Written by Russell T. Davies. Aired 23 April 2005 on BBC, accessed 2018 on iTunes.

Doctor Who, Season 2 (revived series), episode 4, "The Girl in the Fireplace." Directed by Euros Lyn. Written by Steven Moffat. Aired 6 May 2006, accessed 2018 on iTunes.

Doctor Who, Season 6 (revived series), episode 13, "The Wedding of River Song." Directed by Jeremy Webb. Written by Steven Moffat. Aired 1 October 2011 on BBC and BBC America.

Doctor Who, Season 9 (revived series), episode 13, "The Husbands of River Song." Directed by Douglas Mackinnon. Written by Steven Moffat. Aired 25 December 2015 on BBC and BBC America.

Doctor Who, Season 11 (revived series), episode 0, "Twice Upon a Time." Directed by Rachel Talalay. Written by Steven Moffat. Aired 25 December 2017 on BBC and BBC America.

Star Trek

Star Trek, season 1, episode 10, "The Corbomite Maneuver." Directed by Joseph Sargent. Written by Jerry Sohl. Aired 10 November 1966 on NBC, accessed 2018 on Netflix.

Star Trek: The Next Generation, season 1, episode 24, "Conspiracy." Directed by Cliff Bole. Written by Tracy Tormé. Aired 7 May 1988 in syndication, accessed 2018 on Netflix.

Star Trek: The Next Generation, season 2, episode 18, "Up the Long Ladder." Directed by Winrich Kolbe. Written by Melinda M. Snodgrass. Aired 20 May 1989 in syndication, accessed 2018 on Netflix.

Star Trek: The Next Generation, season 4, episode 2, "Family." Directed by Les Landau. Written by Ronald D. Moore. Aired 29 September 1990 in syndication, accessed 2018 on Netflix.

Star Trek: The Next Generation, season 6, episode 4, "Relics." Directed by Alexander Singer. Written by Ronald D. Moore. Aired 10 October 1992 in syndication, accessed 2018 on Netflix.

Star Trek: Deep Space Nine, season 1, episode 1, "Emissary." Directed by David Carson. Written by Rick Berman and Michael Piller. Aired 3 January 1993 in syndication, accessed 2018 on Netflix.

Star Trek: Deep Space Nine, season 4, episode 24, "Body Parts." Directed by Avery Brooks. Written by Hans Beimler. Aired 10 June 1996 in syndication, accessed 2018 on Netflix.

Game of Thrones

Game of Thrones, season 1, episode 7, "You Win or You Die." Directed by Daniel Minahan. Written for television by David Benioff and D.B. Weiss, based on *A Song of Ice and Fire* by George R.R. Martin. Aired 29 May 2011 on HBO.

Game of Thrones, season 6, episode 2, "Home." Directed by Jeremy Podeswa. Written for television by Dave Hill., based on *A Song of Ice and Fire* by George R.R. Martin. Aired 1 May 2016 on HBO.

Breaking Bad and Better Call Saul

Breaking Bad, season 1, episode 1, "Pilot." Directed by Vince Gilligan. Written by Vince Gilligan. Aired 20 January 2008 on AMC.

Breaking Bad, season 1, episode 4, "Cancer Man." Directed by Jim McKay. Written by Vince Gilligan. Aired 17 February 2018 on AMC.

Breaking Bad, season 2, episode 2, "Grilled." Directed by Charles Haid. Written by George Mastras. Aired 15 March 2009 on AMC.

Breaking Bad, season 2, episode 3, "Bit by a Dead Bee." Directed by Terry McDonough, Written by Peter Gould. Aired 22 March 2009 on AMC.

Breaking Bad, season 2, episode 5, "Breakage." Directed by Johan Renck. Written by Moira Walley-Becket. Aired 5 April 2009 on AMC.

Breaking Bad, season 2, episode 7, "A No-Rough-Tough-Stuff-Type Deal." Directed by Tim Hunter. Written by Peter Gould. Aired 9 March 2008 on AMC.

Breaking Bad, season 2, episode 12, "Phoenix." Directed by Colin Bucksey. Written by John Shiban. Aired 24 May 2009 on AMC.

Breaking Bad, season 4, episode 10, "Salud." Directed by Michelle MacLaren. Written by Peter Gould and Gennifer Hutchison. Aired 18 September 2011 on AMC.

Breaking Bad, season 4, episode 11, "Crawl Space." Directed by Scott Winant. Written by Sam Catlin and George Mastras. Aired 25 September 2011 on AMC.

Breaking Bad, season 4, episode 13 "Face Off." Directed by Vince Gilligan. Written by Vince Gilligan. Aired 9 October 2011 on AMC.

Breaking Bad, season 5, episode 1, "Live Free or Die." Directed by Michael Slovis. Written by Vince Gilligan. Aired 15 July 2012 on AMC.

Breaking Bad, season 5, episode 15, "Granite State." Directed by Peter Gould. Written by Peter Gould. Aired 22 September 2013 on AMC.

Breaking Bad, season 5, episode 16, "Felina." Directed by Vince Gilligan. Written by Vince Gilligan. Aired 29 September 2013 on AMC.

Better Call Saul, season 1, episode 9, "Pimento." Directed by Thomas Schnauz. Written by Thomas Schnuz. Aired 30 March 2015 on AMC.

Better Call Saul, season 2, episode 1, "Switch." Directed by Thomas Schnauz. Written by Thomas Schnauz. Aired 15 February 2016 on AMC.

The Walking Dead and Fear The Walking Dead

The Walking Dead, season 2, episode 4, "Cherokee Rose." Directed by Billy Gierhart. Written by Evan Reilly, based on the graphic novel series, *The Walking Dead* by Robert Kirkman. Aired 6 November 2011 on AMC.

The Walking Dead, season 2, episode 8, "Nebraska." Directed by Clark Johnson. Written by Evan Reilly, based on the graphic novel series, *The Walking Dead* by Robert Kirkman. Aired 12 February 2012 on AMC.

The Walking Dead, season 2, episode 9, "Triggerfinger." Directed by Billy Gierhart. Written by David Leslie Johnson, based on the graphic novel series *The Walking Dead* by Robert Kirkman. Aired 19 February 2012 on AMC.

The Walking Dead, season 3, episode 13, "Arrow on the Doorpost." Directed by David Boyd. Written by Ryan C. Coleman, based on the graphic novel series, *The Walking Dead* by Robert Kirkman. Aired 10 March 2013 on AMC.

The Walking Dead, season 4, episode 1, "30 Days Without an Accident." Directed by Greg Nicotero. Written by Scott M. Gimple, based on the graphic novel series, *The Walking Dead* by Robert Kirkman. Aired 13 October 2013 on AMC.

The Walking Dead, season 4, episode 8, "Too Far Gone." Directed by Ernest Dickerson. Written by Seth Hoffman, based on the graphic novel series, *The Walking Dead* by Robert Kirkman. Aired 1 December 2013 on AMC.

The Walking Dead, season 4, episode 12, "Still." Directed by Julius Ramsay. Written by Angela Kang, based on the graphic novel series, *The Walking Dead* by Robert Kirkman. Aired 2 March 2014 on AMC.

The Walking Dead, season 7, episode 5, "Go Getters." Directed by Darnell Martin. Written by Channing Powell, based on the graphic novel series, *The Walking Dead* by Robert Kirkman. Aired 20 November 2016 on AMC.

The Walking Dead, season 7, episode 14, "The Other Side." Directed by Michael E. Satrazemis. Written by Angela Kang, based on the graphic novel series, *The Walking Dead* by Robert Kirkman. Aired 19 March 2017 on AMC.

Fear the Walking Dead, season 2, episode 9, "Los Muertos." Directed by Deborah Chow. Written by Alan Page. Aired 28 August 2016 on AMC.

Fear the Walking Dead, season 4, episode 11, "The Code." Directed by Tara Nicole Weyr. Written by Andrew Chambliss and Alex Delyle. Aired 26 August 2018 on AMC.

Fear the Walking Dead, season 4, episode 12, "Weak," Directed by Colman Domingo. Written by Kalinda Vazquez. Aired 2 September 2018 on AMC.

Fear the Walking Dead, season 4, episode 13, "Blackjack." Directed by Sharat Raju. Written by Ian Goldberg and Richard Naing. Aired 9 September 2018 on AMC.

Fear the Walking Dead, season 4, episode 14, "MM 54." Directed by Lou Diamond Phillips. Written by Anna Fishko and Shintaro Shimosawa. Aired 16 September 2018 on AMC.

Fear the Walking Dead, season 4, episode 15, "I Lose People…" Directed by David Barrett. Written by Kalinda Vazquez. Aired 23 September 2018 on AMC.

Fear the Walking Dead, season 4, episode 16, "…I Lose Myself." Directed by Michael E. Satrazemis. Written by Andrew Chambliss and Ian Goldberg. Aired 30 September 2018 on AMC.

Jessica Jones

Marvel's Jessica Jones, season 1, episode 1, "AKA Ladies Night." Directed by S.J. Clarkson. Written by Melissa Rosenberg, based on the Marvel comic book character created by Brian Michael Bendis and Michael Gaydos. Released on Netflix 20 November 2015.

Marvel's Jessica Jones, season 1, episode 8, "AKA WWJD." Directed by Simon Cellan Jones. Written by Scott Reynolds, based on the Marvel comic book character created by Brian Michael Bendis and Michael Gaydos. Released on Netflix 20 November 2015.

Marvel's Jessica Jones, season 2, episode 2, "AKA Freak Accident." Directed by Minkie Spiro. Written by Aïda Mashak Croal, based on the Marvel comic book character created by Brian Michael Bendis and Michael Gaydos.

Marvel's Jessica Jones, season 2, episode 9, "AKA Shark in the Bathtub, Monster in the Bed." Directed by Rosemary Rodriguez. Written by Jenny Klein, based on the Marvel comic book character created by Brian Michael Bendis and Michael Gaydos. Released on Netflix 8 March 2018.

VIDEO GAMES

The Witcher 3: Wild Hunt. Directed by Konrad Tomaszkiewicz, Mateusz Kanik, and Sebastian Stepien. Written by Marcin Blacha, based on *The Witcher* book series by Andrzej Sapkowski. Art by Marian Chomiak. Warsaw, Poland, CD Projekt Red, 2015.

Fallout 4. Directed by Todd Howard. Written by Emil Pagliarulo. Art by Istvan Pely. Rockville, Maryland, Bethesda Softworks, 2015.

Leisure Suit Larry in the Land of the Lounge Lizards. Created by Al Lowe. Bellevue, Washington, Sierra Entertainment, 1987.

Grand Theft Auto. Created by David Jones and Mike Dailly. New York, Rockstar Games, 1997–2013.

EverQuest Produced by Brad McQuaid. Designed by Steve Clover, Brad McQuaid and William Trost. Art by Rosie Rappaport. San Diego, California, daybreak Game Company, 1999.

INTERVIEWS

Russell, Will. Phone interview. 9 July 2018.

Kaplan, Andrew. In-person interview. 22 July 2018.

Giraldez, Brandon. Phone interview 25 July 2018.

Cioletti, Thomas. In-person interview. 21 August 2018.

De Young, Laura. Skype interview. 2 December 2018.

Maddock, Robin. Skype interview. 2 December 2018.

Ormiston, Craig. Video conference interview. 4 October 2018.

Colloton, Eddy. Video conference interview. 4 October 2018.

Ferencz, Brett. Phone interview. 19 November 2018.

Peal, Ben. Phone interview. 13 December 2018.

ABOUT THE AUTHOR

Jeff Cioletti's tenure in liquid literacy has exposed him to some of the best libations the world has to offer and given him access to the producers and purveyors of such fine refreshments. He combines his love of drink with a passion for travel and one usually involves the other. He is the editor in chief of the American Craft Spirits Association's digital publications. Before that, he served for fourteen years as an editor at *Beverage World* magazine, including eight years as editor in chief. He's also the author of the books *The Drinkable Globe*, *SakePedia*, *The Year of Drinking Adventurously* and *Beer FAQ*. Jeff is the founder of DrinkableGlobe.com and host of The Drinkable Globe Podcast and has been a frequent contributor to publications including *Artisan Spirit Magazine, Beverage Media, BevNet, Beverage Industry, The Takeout, SevenFifty Daily,* and *CraftBeer.com.* Additionally, he's certified as an International Kikisake-shi (sake sommelier) by Sake Service Institute International and is the winner of four North American Guild of Beer Writers awards.

Mango Publishing, established in 2014, publishes an eclectic list of books by diverse authors—both new and established voices—on topics ranging from business, personal growth, women's empowerment, LGBTQ studies, health, and spirituality to history, popular culture, time management, decluttering, lifestyle, mental wellness, aging, and sustainable living. We were recently named 2019's #1 fastest growing independent publisher by *Publishers Weekly*. Our success is driven by our main goal, which is to publish high quality books that will entertain readers as well as make a positive difference in their lives.

Our readers are our most important resource; we value your input, suggestions, and ideas. We'd love to hear from you—after all, we are publishing books for you!

Please stay in touch with us and follow us at:

Facebook: Mango Publishing
Twitter: @MangoPublishing
Instagram: @MangoPublishing
LinkedIn: Mango Publishing
Pinterest: Mango Publishing

Sign up for our newsletter at www.mango.bz and receive a free book!

Join us on Mango's journey to reinvent publishing, one book at a time.